Cigar Tasting

INFORMATION

NAME

ADDRESS

E-MAIL ADDRESS

WEBSITE

PHONE   **FAX**

EMERGENCY CONTACT PERSON

PHONE   **FAX**

Cigar Tasting Journal

NAME OF CIGAR

DATE   **ORIGIN**

BRAND   **TYPE**

WRAPPER   **FILLER**

SAMPLED   **LENGTH / RING SIZE**

> PLACE CIGAR LABLE HERE

FLAVOR

- ☐ BITTER
- ☐ SPICY
- ☐ WOODY
- ☐ EARTHY
- ☐ NUTTY
- ☐ CREAMY
- ☐ CHOCOLATE
- ☐ TOFFEE
- ☐ SWEET
- ☐ FLORAL
- ☐ FRUITY
- ☐ SOUR
- ☐ HERBAL
- ☐ OILY
- ☐ LEATHER

FLAVOR STRENGTH

① ② ③ ④ ⑤ ⑥ ⑦ ⑧ ⑨ ⑩

NOTES

....
....
....

WOULD YOU TRY AGAIN?

☐ YES   ☐ NO

OVERALL RATING

⭐ ⭐ ⭐ ⭐ ⭐

Cigar Tasting Journal

NAME OF CIGAR

DATE   **ORIGIN**

BRAND   **TYPE**

WRAPPER   **FILLER**

SAMPLED   **LENGTH / RING SIZE**

PLACE CIGAR LABLE HERE

FLAVOR

☐ BITTER   ☐ CREAMY   ☐ FRUITY
☐ SPICY   ☐ CHOCOLATE   ☐ SOUR
☐ WOODY   ☐ TOFFEE   ☐ HERBAL
☐ EARTHY   ☐ SWEET   ☐ OILY
☐ NUTTY   ☐ FLORAL   ☐ LEATHER

FLAVOR STRENGTH

① ② ③ ④ ⑤ ⑥ ⑦ ⑧ ⑨ ⑩

NOTES

WOULD YOU TRY AGAIN?   OVERALL RATING

☐ YES   ☐ NO   ★ ★ ★ ★ ★

Cigar Tasting Journal

NAME OF CIGAR

DATE   **ORIGIN**

BRAND   **TYPE**

WRAPPER   **FILLER**

SAMPLED   **LENGTH / RING SIZE**

PLACE CIGAR LABLE HERE

FLAVOR

- ☐ BITTER
- ☐ SPICY
- ☐ WOODY
- ☐ EARTHY
- ☐ NUTTY

- ☐ CREAMY
- ☐ CHOCOLATE
- ☐ TOFFEE
- ☐ SWEET
- ☐ FLORAL

- ☐ FRUITY
- ☐ SOUR
- ☐ HERBAL
- ☐ OILY
- ☐ LEATHER

FLAVOR STRENGTH

① ② ③ ④ ⑤ ⑥ ⑦ ⑧ ⑨ ⑩

NOTES

....
....
....

WOULD YOU TRY AGAIN?

☐ YES   ☐ NO

OVERALL RATING

★ ★ ★ ★ ★

Cigar Tasting Journal

NAME OF CIGAR

DATE **ORIGIN**

BRAND **TYPE**

WRAPPER **FILLER**

SAMPLED **LENGTH / RING SIZE**

PLACE CIGAR LABLE HERE

FLAVOR

- [ ] BITTER
- [ ] SPICY
- [ ] WOODY
- [ ] EARTHY
- [ ] NUTTY

- [ ] CREAMY
- [ ] CHOCOLATE
- [ ] TOFFEE
- [ ] SWEET
- [ ] FLORAL

- [ ] FRUITY
- [ ] SOUR
- [ ] HERBAL
- [ ] OILY
- [ ] LEATHER

FLAVOR STRENGTH

(1) (2) (3) (4) (5) (6) (7) (8) (9) (10)

NOTES

....
....
....

WOULD YOU TRY AGAIN?

- [ ] YES
- [ ] NO

OVERALL RATING

★ ★ ★ ★ ★

Cigar Tasting Journal

NAME OF CIGAR

DATE   **ORIGIN**

BRAND   **TYPE**

WRAPPER   **FILLER**

SAMPLED   **LENGTH / RING SIZE**

PLACE CIGAR LABLE HERE

FLAVOR

☐ BITTER   ☐ CREAMY   ☐ FRUITY
☐ SPICY   ☐ CHOCOLATE   ☐ SOUR
☐ WOODY   ☐ TOFFEE   ☐ HERBAL
☐ EARTHY   ☐ SWEET   ☐ OILY
☐ NUTTY   ☐ FLORAL   ☐ LEATHER

FLAVOR STRENGTH

① ② ③ ④ ⑤ ⑥ ⑦ ⑧ ⑨ ⑩

NOTES

....
....
....

WOULD YOU TRY AGAIN?

☐ YES   ☐ NO

OVERALL RATING

★ ★ ★ ★ ★

Cigar Tasting Journal

NAME OF CIGAR

DATE

ORIGIN

BRAND

TYPE

WRAPPER

FILLER

SAMPLED

LENGTH / RING SIZE

PLACE CIGAR LABLE HERE

FLAVOR

- [ ] BITTER
- [ ] SPICY
- [ ] WOODY
- [ ] EARTHY
- [ ] NUTTY
- [ ] CREAMY
- [ ] CHOCOLATE
- [ ] TOFFEE
- [ ] SWEET
- [ ] FLORAL
- [ ] FRUITY
- [ ] SOUR
- [ ] HERBAL
- [ ] OILY
- [ ] LEATHER

FLAVOR STRENGTH

(1) (2) (3) (4) (5) (6) (7) (8) (9) (10)

NOTES

....
....
....

WOULD YOU TRY AGAIN?

- [ ] YES
- [ ] NO

OVERALL RATING

★ ★ ★ ★ ★

Cigar Tasting Journal

NAME OF CIGAR

DATE   **ORIGIN**

BRAND   **TYPE**

WRAPPER   **FILLER**

SAMPLED   **LENGTH / RING SIZE**

PLACE CIGAR LABLE HERE

FLAVOR

☐ BITTER   ☐ CREAMY   ☐ FRUITY
☐ SPICY   ☐ CHOCOLATE   ☐ SOUR
☐ WOODY   ☐ TOFFEE   ☐ HERBAL
☐ EARTHY   ☐ SWEET   ☐ OILY
☐ NUTTY   ☐ FLORAL   ☐ LEATHER

FLAVOR STRENGTH

① ② ③ ④ ⑤ ⑥ ⑦ ⑧ ⑨ ⑩

NOTES

....
....
....

WOULD YOU TRY AGAIN?

☐ YES   ☐ NO

OVERALL RATING

★ ★ ★ ★ ★

Cigar Tasting Journal

NAME OF CIGAR

DATE   **ORIGIN**

BRAND   **TYPE**

WRAPPER   **FILLER**

SAMPLED   **LENGTH / RING SIZE**

PLACE CIGAR LABLE HERE

FLAVOR

- [ ] BITTER
- [ ] SPICY
- [ ] WOODY
- [ ] EARTHY
- [ ] NUTTY

- [ ] CREAMY
- [ ] CHOCOLATE
- [ ] TOFFEE
- [ ] SWEET
- [ ] FLORAL

- [ ] FRUITY
- [ ] SOUR
- [ ] HERBAL
- [ ] OILY
- [ ] LEATHER

FLAVOR STRENGTH

(1) (2) (3) (4) (5) (6) (7) (8) (9) (10)

NOTES

....
....
....

WOULD YOU TRY AGAIN?   **OVERALL RATING**

- [ ] YES   - [ ] NO   ★ ★ ★ ★ ★

Cigar Tasting Journal

NAME OF CIGAR

DATE   **ORIGIN**

BRAND   **TYPE**

WRAPPER   **FILLER**

SAMPLED   **LENGTH / RING SIZE**

PLACE CIGAR LABLE HERE

FLAVOR

- ☐ BITTER
- ☐ SPICY
- ☐ WOODY
- ☐ EARTHY
- ☐ NUTTY

- ☐ CREAMY
- ☐ CHOCOLATE
- ☐ TOFFEE
- ☐ SWEET
- ☐ FLORAL

- ☐ FRUITY
- ☐ SOUR
- ☐ HERBAL
- ☐ OILY
- ☐ LEATHER

FLAVOR STRENGTH

① ② ③ ④ ⑤ ⑥ ⑦ ⑧ ⑨ ⑩

NOTES

....
....
....

WOULD YOU TRY AGAIN?

☐ YES   ☐ NO

OVERALL RATING

★ ★ ★ ★ ★

Cigar Tasting Journal

NAME OF CIGAR

DATE   **ORIGIN**

BRAND   **TYPE**

WRAPPER   **FILLER**

SAMPLED   **LENGTH / RING SIZE**

PLACE CIGAR LABLE HERE

FLAVOR

☐ BITTER   ☐ CREAMY   ☐ FRUITY
☐ SPICY   ☐ CHOCOLATE   ☐ SOUR
☐ WOODY   ☐ TOFFEE   ☐ HERBAL
☐ EARTHY   ☐ SWEET   ☐ OILY
☐ NUTTY   ☐ FLORAL   ☐ LEATHER

FLAVOR STRENGTH

① ② ③ ④ ⑤ ⑥ ⑦ ⑧ ⑨ ⑩

NOTES

....
....
....

WOULD YOU TRY AGAIN?   **OVERALL RATING**

☐ YES   ☐ NO   ★ ★ ★ ★ ★

Cigar Tasting Journal

NAME OF CIGAR

DATE | **ORIGIN**

BRAND | **TYPE**

WRAPPER | **FILLER**

SAMPLED | **LENGTH / RING SIZE**

PLACE CIGAR LABLE HERE

FLAVOR

- [ ] BITTER
- [ ] SPICY
- [ ] WOODY
- [ ] EARTHY
- [ ] NUTTY
- [ ] CREAMY
- [ ] CHOCOLATE
- [ ] TOFFEE
- [ ] SWEET
- [ ] FLORAL
- [ ] FRUITY
- [ ] SOUR
- [ ] HERBAL
- [ ] OILY
- [ ] LEATHER

FLAVOR STRENGTH

(1) (2) (3) (4) (5) (6) (7) (8) (9) (10)

NOTES

....
....
....

WOULD YOU TRY AGAIN? | **OVERALL RATING**

- [ ] YES
- [ ] NO

★ ★ ★ ★ ★

Cigar Tasting Journal

NAME OF CIGAR

DATE   **ORIGIN**

BRAND   **TYPE**

WRAPPER   **FILLER**

SAMPLED   **LENGTH / RING SIZE**

PLACE CIGAR LABLE HERE

FLAVOR

- [ ] BITTER
- [ ] SPICY
- [ ] WOODY
- [ ] EARTHY
- [ ] NUTTY

- [ ] CREAMY
- [ ] CHOCOLATE
- [ ] TOFFEE
- [ ] SWEET
- [ ] FLORAL

- [ ] FRUITY
- [ ] SOUR
- [ ] HERBAL
- [ ] OILY
- [ ] LEATHER

FLAVOR STRENGTH

(1) (2) (3) (4) (5) (6) (7) (8) (9) (10)

NOTES

....
....
....

WOULD YOU TRY AGAIN?

- [ ] YES
- [ ] NO

OVERALL RATING

★ ★ ★ ★ ★

Cigar Tasting Journal

NAME OF CIGAR

DATE　　　　　　　　　　　　**ORIGIN**

BRAND　　　　　　　　　　　　**TYPE**

WRAPPER　　　　　　　　　　**FILLER**

SAMPLED　　　　　　　　　　**LENGTH / RING SIZE**

PLACE CIGAR LABLE HERE

FLAVOR

☐ BITTER　　☐ CREAMY　　☐ FRUITY
☐ SPICY　　☐ CHOCOLATE　　☐ SOUR
☐ WOODY　　☐ TOFFEE　　☐ HERBAL
☐ EARTHY　　☐ SWEET　　☐ OILY
☐ NUTTY　　☐ FLORAL　　☐ LEATHER

FLAVOR STRENGTH

① ② ③ ④ ⑤ ⑥ ⑦ ⑧ ⑨ ⑩

NOTES

....
....
....

WOULD YOU TRY AGAIN?

☐ YES　　☐ NO

OVERALL RATING

★ ★ ★ ★ ★

Cigar Tasting Journal

NAME OF CIGAR

DATE   **ORIGIN**

BRAND   **TYPE**

WRAPPER   **FILLER**

SAMPLED   **LENGTH / RING SIZE**

PLACE CIGAR LABLE HERE

FLAVOR

☐ BITTER   ☐ CREAMY   ☐ FRUITY

☐ SPICY   ☐ CHOCOLATE   ☐ SOUR

☐ WOODY   ☐ TOFFEE   ☐ HERBAL

☐ EARTHY   ☐ SWEET   ☐ OILY

☐ NUTTY   ☐ FLORAL   ☐ LEATHER

FLAVOR STRENGTH

① ② ③ ④ ⑤ ⑥ ⑦ ⑧ ⑨ ⑩

NOTES

....

....

....

WOULD YOU TRY AGAIN?   **OVERALL RATING**

☐ YES   ☐ NO   ★ ★ ★ ★ ★

Cigar Tasting Journal

NAME OF CIGAR

DATE   **ORIGIN**

BRAND   **TYPE**

WRAPPER   **FILLER**

SAMPLED   **LENGTH / RING SIZE**

PLACE CIGAR LABLE HERE

FLAVOR

- [ ] BITTER
- [ ] SPICY
- [ ] WOODY
- [ ] EARTHY
- [ ] NUTTY

- [ ] CREAMY
- [ ] CHOCOLATE
- [ ] TOFFEE
- [ ] SWEET
- [ ] FLORAL

- [ ] FRUITY
- [ ] SOUR
- [ ] HERBAL
- [ ] OILY
- [ ] LEATHER

FLAVOR STRENGTH

(1) (2) (3) (4) (5) (6) (7) (8) (9) (10)

NOTES

WOULD YOU TRY AGAIN?

- [ ] YES
- [ ] NO

OVERALL RATING

☆ ☆ ☆ ☆ ☆

Cigar Tasting Journal

NAME OF CIGAR

DATE   **ORIGIN**

BRAND   **TYPE**

WRAPPER   **FILLER**

SAMPLED   **LENGTH / RING SIZE**

PLACE CIGAR LABLE HERE

FLAVOR

- ☐ BITTER
- ☐ SPICY
- ☐ WOODY
- ☐ EARTHY
- ☐ NUTTY

- ☐ CREAMY
- ☐ CHOCOLATE
- ☐ TOFFEE
- ☐ SWEET
- ☐ FLORAL

- ☐ FRUITY
- ☐ SOUR
- ☐ HERBAL
- ☐ OILY
- ☐ LEATHER

FLAVOR STRENGTH

① ② ③ ④ ⑤ ⑥ ⑦ ⑧ ⑨ ⑩

NOTES

....
....
....

WOULD YOU TRY AGAIN?   **OVERALL RATING**

☐ YES   ☐ NO   ★ ★ ★ ★ ★

Cigar Tasting Journal

NAME OF CIGAR

DATE   **ORIGIN**

BRAND   **TYPE**

WRAPPER   **FILLER**

SAMPLED   **LENGTH / RING SIZE**

PLACE CIGAR LABLE HERE

FLAVOR

☐ BITTER   ☐ CREAMY   ☐ FRUITY
☐ SPICY   ☐ CHOCOLATE   ☐ SOUR
☐ WOODY   ☐ TOFFEE   ☐ HERBAL
☐ EARTHY   ☐ SWEET   ☐ OILY
☐ NUTTY   ☐ FLORAL   ☐ LEATHER

FLAVOR STRENGTH

① ② ③ ④ ⑤ ⑥ ⑦ ⑧ ⑨ ⑩

NOTES

WOULD YOU TRY AGAIN?

☐ YES   ☐ NO

OVERALL RATING

★ ★ ★ ★ ★

Cigar Tasting Journal

NAME OF CIGAR

DATE   **ORIGIN**

BRAND   **TYPE**

WRAPPER   **FILLER**

SAMPLED   **LENGTH / RING SIZE**

PLACE CIGAR LABLE HERE

FLAVOR

☐ BITTER   ☐ CREAMY   ☐ FRUITY
☐ SPICY   ☐ CHOCOLATE   ☐ SOUR
☐ WOODY   ☐ TOFFEE   ☐ HERBAL
☐ EARTHY   ☐ SWEET   ☐ OILY
☐ NUTTY   ☐ FLORAL   ☐ LEATHER

FLAVOR STRENGTH

① ② ③ ④ ⑤ ⑥ ⑦ ⑧ ⑨ ⑩

NOTES

....
....
....

WOULD YOU TRY AGAIN?   **OVERALL RATING**

☐ YES   ☐ NO   ☆ ☆ ☆ ☆ ☆

Cigar Tasting Journal

NAME OF CIGAR

DATE   **ORIGIN**

BRAND   **TYPE**

WRAPPER   **FILLER**

SAMPLED   **LENGTH / RING SIZE**

PLACE CIGAR LABLE HERE

FLAVOR

- ☐ BITTER
- ☐ SPICY
- ☐ WOODY
- ☐ EARTHY
- ☐ NUTTY
- ☐ CREAMY
- ☐ CHOCOLATE
- ☐ TOFFEE
- ☐ SWEET
- ☐ FLORAL
- ☐ FRUITY
- ☐ SOUR
- ☐ HERBAL
- ☐ OILY
- ☐ LEATHER

FLAVOR STRENGTH

① ② ③ ④ ⑤ ⑥ ⑦ ⑧ ⑨ ⑩

NOTES

WOULD YOU TRY AGAIN?

☐ YES   ☐ NO

OVERALL RATING

★ ★ ★ ★ ★

Cigar Tasting Journal

NAME OF CIGAR

DATE **ORIGIN**

BRAND **TYPE**

WRAPPER **FILLER**

SAMPLED **LENGTH / RING SIZE**

PLACE CIGAR LABLE HERE

FLAVOR

- ☐ BITTER
- ☐ SPICY
- ☐ WOODY
- ☐ EARTHY
- ☐ NUTTY
- ☐ CREAMY
- ☐ CHOCOLATE
- ☐ TOFFEE
- ☐ SWEET
- ☐ FLORAL
- ☐ FRUITY
- ☐ SOUR
- ☐ HERBAL
- ☐ OILY
- ☐ LEATHER

FLAVOR STRENGTH

① ② ③ ④ ⑤ ⑥ ⑦ ⑧ ⑨ ⑩

NOTES

....
....
....

WOULD YOU TRY AGAIN?
☐ YES ☐ NO

OVERALL RATING
★ ★ ★ ★ ★

Cigar Tasting Journal

NAME OF CIGAR

DATE   **ORIGIN**

BRAND   **TYPE**

WRAPPER   **FILLER**

SAMPLED   **LENGTH / RING SIZE**

PLACE CIGAR LABLE HERE

FLAVOR

- [ ] BITTER
- [ ] SPICY
- [ ] WOODY
- [ ] EARTHY
- [ ] NUTTY
- [ ] CREAMY
- [ ] CHOCOLATE
- [ ] TOFFEE
- [ ] SWEET
- [ ] FLORAL
- [ ] FRUITY
- [ ] SOUR
- [ ] HERBAL
- [ ] OILY
- [ ] LEATHER

FLAVOR STRENGTH

(1) (2) (3) (4) (5) (6) (7) (8) (9) (10)

NOTES

....
....
....

WOULD YOU TRY AGAIN?

- [ ] YES
- [ ] NO

OVERALL RATING

★ ★ ★ ★ ★

Cigar Tasting Journal

NAME OF CIGAR

DATE   **ORIGIN**

BRAND   **TYPE**

WRAPPER   **FILLER**

SAMPLED   **LENGTH / RING SIZE**

PLACE CIGAR LABLE HERE

FLAVOR

- [ ] BITTER
- [ ] SPICY
- [ ] WOODY
- [ ] EARTHY
- [ ] NUTTY

- [ ] CREAMY
- [ ] CHOCOLATE
- [ ] TOFFEE
- [ ] SWEET
- [ ] FLORAL

- [ ] FRUITY
- [ ] SOUR
- [ ] HERBAL
- [ ] OILY
- [ ] LEATHER

FLAVOR STRENGTH

① ② ③ ④ ⑤ ⑥ ⑦ ⑧ ⑨ ⑩

NOTES

....
....
....

WOULD YOU TRY AGAIN?
- [ ] YES
- [ ] NO

OVERALL RATING
★ ★ ★ ★ ★

Cigar Tasting Journal

NAME OF CIGAR

DATE   **ORIGIN**

BRAND   **TYPE**

WRAPPER   **FILLER**

SAMPLED   **LENGTH / RING SIZE**

PLACE CIGAR LABLE HERE

FLAVOR

☐ BITTER   ☐ CREAMY   ☐ FRUITY
☐ SPICY   ☐ CHOCOLATE   ☐ SOUR
☐ WOODY   ☐ TOFFEE   ☐ HERBAL
☐ EARTHY   ☐ SWEET   ☐ OILY
☐ NUTTY   ☐ FLORAL   ☐ LEATHER

FLAVOR STRENGTH

① ② ③ ④ ⑤ ⑥ ⑦ ⑧ ⑨ ⑩

NOTES

....
....
....

WOULD YOU TRY AGAIN?

☐ YES   ☐ NO

OVERALL RATING

★ ★ ★ ★ ★

Cigar Tasting Journal

NAME OF CIGAR

DATE   **ORIGIN**

BRAND   **TYPE**

WRAPPER   **FILLER**

SAMPLED   **LENGTH / RING SIZE**

PLACE CIGAR LABLE HERE

FLAVOR

- ☐ BITTER
- ☐ SPICY
- ☐ WOODY
- ☐ EARTHY
- ☐ NUTTY
- ☐ CREAMY
- ☐ CHOCOLATE
- ☐ TOFFEE
- ☐ SWEET
- ☐ FLORAL
- ☐ FRUITY
- ☐ SOUR
- ☐ HERBAL
- ☐ OILY
- ☐ LEATHER

FLAVOR STRENGTH

① ② ③ ④ ⑤ ⑥ ⑦ ⑧ ⑨ ⑩

NOTES

....

....

....

WOULD YOU TRY AGAIN?

☐ YES   ☐ NO

OVERALL RATING

★ ★ ★ ★ ★

Cigar Tasting Journal

NAME OF CIGAR

DATE   **ORIGIN**

BRAND   **TYPE**

WRAPPER   **FILLER**

SAMPLED   **LENGTH / RING SIZE**

PLACE CIGAR LABLE HERE

FLAVOR

☐ BITTER   ☐ CREAMY   ☐ FRUITY
☐ SPICY   ☐ CHOCOLATE   ☐ SOUR
☐ WOODY   ☐ TOFFEE   ☐ HERBAL
☐ EARTHY   ☐ SWEET   ☐ OILY
☐ NUTTY   ☐ FLORAL   ☐ LEATHER

FLAVOR STRENGTH

① ② ③ ④ ⑤ ⑥ ⑦ ⑧ ⑨ ⑩

NOTES

....
....
....

WOULD YOU TRY AGAIN?   **OVERALL RATING**

☐ YES   ☐ NO   ★ ★ ★ ★ ★

Cigar Tasting Journal

NAME OF CIGAR

DATE   **ORIGIN**

BRAND   **TYPE**

WRAPPER   **FILLER**

SAMPLED   **LENGTH / RING SIZE**

PLACE CIGAR LABLE HERE

FLAVOR

☐ BITTER   ☐ CREAMY   ☐ FRUITY
☐ SPICY   ☐ CHOCOLATE   ☐ SOUR
☐ WOODY   ☐ TOFFEE   ☐ HERBAL
☐ EARTHY   ☐ SWEET   ☐ OILY
☐ NUTTY   ☐ FLORAL   ☐ LEATHER

FLAVOR STRENGTH

① ② ③ ④ ⑤ ⑥ ⑦ ⑧ ⑨ ⑩

NOTES

....
....
....

WOULD YOU TRY AGAIN?   **OVERALL RATING**

☐ YES   ☐ NO   ★ ★ ★ ★ ★

Cigar Tasting Journal

NAME OF CIGAR

DATE   **ORIGIN**

BRAND   **TYPE**

WRAPPER   **FILLER**

SAMPLED   **LENGTH / RING SIZE**

PLACE CIGAR LABLE HERE

FLAVOR

- [ ] BITTER
- [ ] SPICY
- [ ] WOODY
- [ ] EARTHY
- [ ] NUTTY
- [ ] CREAMY
- [ ] CHOCOLATE
- [ ] TOFFEE
- [ ] SWEET
- [ ] FLORAL
- [ ] FRUITY
- [ ] SOUR
- [ ] HERBAL
- [ ] OILY
- [ ] LEATHER

FLAVOR STRENGTH

(1) (2) (3) (4) (5) (6) (7) (8) (9) (10)

NOTES

....
....
....

WOULD YOU TRY AGAIN?

- [ ] YES
- [ ] NO

OVERALL RATING

⭐ ⭐ ⭐ ⭐ ⭐

Cigar Tasting Journal

NAME OF CIGAR

DATE   **ORIGIN**

BRAND   **TYPE**

WRAPPER   **FILLER**

SAMPLED   **LENGTH / RING SIZE**

> PLACE CIGAR LABLE HERE

FLAVOR

- ☐ BITTER
- ☐ SPICY
- ☐ WOODY
- ☐ EARTHY
- ☐ NUTTY

- ☐ CREAMY
- ☐ CHOCOLATE
- ☐ TOFFEE
- ☐ SWEET
- ☐ FLORAL

- ☐ FRUITY
- ☐ SOUR
- ☐ HERBAL
- ☐ OILY
- ☐ LEATHER

FLAVOR STRENGTH

① ② ③ ④ ⑤ ⑥ ⑦ ⑧ ⑨ ⑩

NOTES

....

....

....

WOULD YOU TRY AGAIN?

☐ YES   ☐ NO

OVERALL RATING

★ ★ ★ ★ ★

Cigar Tasting Journal

NAME OF CIGAR

DATE   **ORIGIN**

BRAND   **TYPE**

WRAPPER   **FILLER**

SAMPLED   **LENGTH / RING SIZE**

PLACE CIGAR LABLE HERE

FLAVOR

☐ BITTER   ☐ CREAMY   ☐ FRUITY
☐ SPICY   ☐ CHOCOLATE   ☐ SOUR
☐ WOODY   ☐ TOFFEE   ☐ HERBAL
☐ EARTHY   ☐ SWEET   ☐ OILY
☐ NUTTY   ☐ FLORAL   ☐ LEATHER

FLAVOR STRENGTH

① ② ③ ④ ⑤ ⑥ ⑦ ⑧ ⑨ ⑩

NOTES

....
....
....

WOULD YOU TRY AGAIN?   OVERALL RATING

☐ YES   ☐ NO   ☆ ☆ ☆ ☆ ☆

Cigar Tasting Journal

NAME OF CIGAR

DATE   **ORIGIN**

BRAND   **TYPE**

WRAPPER   **FILLER**

SAMPLED   **LENGTH / RING SIZE**

PLACE CIGAR LABLE HERE

FLAVOR

- [ ] BITTER
- [ ] SPICY
- [ ] WOODY
- [ ] EARTHY
- [ ] NUTTY

- [ ] CREAMY
- [ ] CHOCOLATE
- [ ] TOFFEE
- [ ] SWEET
- [ ] FLORAL

- [ ] FRUITY
- [ ] SOUR
- [ ] HERBAL
- [ ] OILY
- [ ] LEATHER

FLAVOR STRENGTH

(1) (2) (3) (4) (5) (6) (7) (8) (9) (10)

NOTES

....
....
....

WOULD YOU TRY AGAIN?   **OVERALL RATING**

- [ ] YES   - [ ] NO   ★ ★ ★ ★ ★

Cigar Tasting Journal

NAME OF CIGAR

DATE   **ORIGIN**

BRAND   **TYPE**

WRAPPER   **FILLER**

SAMPLED   **LENGTH / RING SIZE**

PLACE CIGAR LABLE HERE

FLAVOR

☐ BITTER   ☐ CREAMY   ☐ FRUITY
☐ SPICY   ☐ CHOCOLATE   ☐ SOUR
☐ WOODY   ☐ TOFFEE   ☐ HERBAL
☐ EARTHY   ☐ SWEET   ☐ OILY
☐ NUTTY   ☐ FLORAL   ☐ LEATHER

FLAVOR STRENGTH

① ② ③ ④ ⑤ ⑥ ⑦ ⑧ ⑨ ⑩

NOTES

....
....
....

WOULD YOU TRY AGAIN?   OVERALL RATING

☐ YES   ☐ NO   ★ ★ ★ ★ ★

Cigar Tasting Journal

NAME OF CIGAR

DATE   **ORIGIN**

BRAND   **TYPE**

WRAPPER   **FILLER**

SAMPLED   **LENGTH / RING SIZE**

PLACE CIGAR LABLE HERE

FLAVOR

☐ BITTER   ☐ CREAMY   ☐ FRUITY

☐ SPICY   ☐ CHOCOLATE   ☐ SOUR

☐ WOODY   ☐ TOFFEE   ☐ HERBAL

☐ EARTHY   ☐ SWEET   ☐ OILY

☐ NUTTY   ☐ FLORAL   ☐ LEATHER

FLAVOR STRENGTH

① ② ③ ④ ⑤ ⑥ ⑦ ⑧ ⑨ ⑩

NOTES

....
....
....

WOULD YOU TRY AGAIN?   **OVERALL RATING**

☐ YES   ☐ NO   ★ ★ ★ ★ ★

Cigar Tasting Journal

NAME OF CIGAR

DATE   **ORIGIN**

BRAND   **TYPE**

WRAPPER   **FILLER**

SAMPLED   **LENGTH / RING SIZE**

PLACE CIGAR LABLE HERE

FLAVOR

- [ ] BITTER
- [ ] SPICY
- [ ] WOODY
- [ ] EARTHY
- [ ] NUTTY
- [ ] CREAMY
- [ ] CHOCOLATE
- [ ] TOFFEE
- [ ] SWEET
- [ ] FLORAL
- [ ] FRUITY
- [ ] SOUR
- [ ] HERBAL
- [ ] OILY
- [ ] LEATHER

FLAVOR STRENGTH

(1) (2) (3) (4) (5) (6) (7) (8) (9) (10)

NOTES

WOULD YOU TRY AGAIN?

- [ ] YES
- [ ] NO

OVERALL RATING

★ ★ ★ ★ ★

Cigar Tasting Journal

NAME OF CIGAR

DATE   **ORIGIN**

BRAND   **TYPE**

WRAPPER   **FILLER**

SAMPLED   **LENGTH / RING SIZE**

PLACE CIGAR LABLE HERE

FLAVOR

- [ ] BITTER
- [ ] SPICY
- [ ] WOODY
- [ ] EARTHY
- [ ] NUTTY

- [ ] CREAMY
- [ ] CHOCOLATE
- [ ] TOFFEE
- [ ] SWEET
- [ ] FLORAL

- [ ] FRUITY
- [ ] SOUR
- [ ] HERBAL
- [ ] OILY
- [ ] LEATHER

FLAVOR STRENGTH

(1) (2) (3) (4) (5) (6) (7) (8) (9) (10)

NOTES

....
....
....

WOULD YOU TRY AGAIN?   **OVERALL RATING**

- [ ] YES   [ ] NO   ★ ★ ★ ★ ★

Cigar Tasting Journal

NAME OF CIGAR

DATE   ORIGIN

BRAND   TYPE

WRAPPER   FILLER

SAMPLED   LENGTH / RING SIZE

PLACE CIGAR LABLE HERE

FLAVOR

- [ ] BITTER
- [ ] SPICY
- [ ] WOODY
- [ ] EARTHY
- [ ] NUTTY
- [ ] CREAMY
- [ ] CHOCOLATE
- [ ] TOFFEE
- [ ] SWEET
- [ ] FLORAL
- [ ] FRUITY
- [ ] SOUR
- [ ] HERBAL
- [ ] OILY
- [ ] LEATHER

FLAVOR STRENGTH

(1) (2) (3) (4) (5) (6) (7) (8) (9) (10)

NOTES

....
....
....

WOULD YOU TRY AGAIN?

- [ ] YES
- [ ] NO

OVERALL RATING

★ ★ ★ ★ ★

Cigar Tasting Journal

NAME OF CIGAR

DATE   **ORIGIN**

BRAND   **TYPE**

WRAPPER   **FILLER**

SAMPLED   **LENGTH / RING SIZE**

PLACE CIGAR LABLE HERE

FLAVOR

- ☐ BITTER
- ☐ SPICY
- ☐ WOODY
- ☐ EARTHY
- ☐ NUTTY
- ☐ CREAMY
- ☐ CHOCOLATE
- ☐ TOFFEE
- ☐ SWEET
- ☐ FLORAL
- ☐ FRUITY
- ☐ SOUR
- ☐ HERBAL
- ☐ OILY
- ☐ LEATHER

FLAVOR STRENGTH

①　②　③　④　⑤　⑥　⑦　⑧　⑨　⑩

NOTES

....
....
....

WOULD YOU TRY AGAIN?

☐ YES   ☐ NO

OVERALL RATING

★ ★ ★ ★ ★

Cigar Tasting Journal

NAME OF CIGAR

DATE   **ORIGIN**

BRAND   **TYPE**

WRAPPER   **FILLER**

SAMPLED   **LENGTH / RING SIZE**

PLACE CIGAR LABLE HERE

FLAVOR

- ☐ BITTER
- ☐ SPICY
- ☐ WOODY
- ☐ EARTHY
- ☐ NUTTY
- ☐ CREAMY
- ☐ CHOCOLATE
- ☐ TOFFEE
- ☐ SWEET
- ☐ FLORAL
- ☐ FRUITY
- ☐ SOUR
- ☐ HERBAL
- ☐ OILY
- ☐ LEATHER

FLAVOR STRENGTH

① ② ③ ④ ⑤ ⑥ ⑦ ⑧ ⑨ ⑩

NOTES

....
....
....

WOULD YOU TRY AGAIN?

☐ YES   ☐ NO

OVERALL RATING

★ ★ ★ ★ ★

Cigar Tasting Journal

NAME OF CIGAR

DATE   **ORIGIN**

BRAND   **TYPE**

WRAPPER   **FILLER**

SAMPLED   **LENGTH / RING SIZE**

PLACE CIGAR LABLE HERE

FLAVOR

- ☐ BITTER
- ☐ SPICY
- ☐ WOODY
- ☐ EARTHY
- ☐ NUTTY

- ☐ CREAMY
- ☐ CHOCOLATE
- ☐ TOFFEE
- ☐ SWEET
- ☐ FLORAL

- ☐ FRUITY
- ☐ SOUR
- ☐ HERBAL
- ☐ OILY
- ☐ LEATHER

FLAVOR STRENGTH

① ② ③ ④ ⑤ ⑥ ⑦ ⑧ ⑨ ⑩

NOTES

....

....

....

WOULD YOU TRY AGAIN?   **OVERALL RATING**

☐ YES   ☐ NO   ★ ★ ★ ★ ★

Cigar Tasting Journal

NAME OF CIGAR

DATE   **ORIGIN**

BRAND   **TYPE**

WRAPPER   **FILLER**

SAMPLED   **LENGTH / RING SIZE**

PLACE CIGAR LABLE HERE

FLAVOR

☐ BITTER   ☐ CREAMY   ☐ FRUITY
☐ SPICY   ☐ CHOCOLATE   ☐ SOUR
☐ WOODY   ☐ TOFFEE   ☐ HERBAL
☐ EARTHY   ☐ SWEET   ☐ OILY
☐ NUTTY   ☐ FLORAL   ☐ LEATHER

FLAVOR STRENGTH

① ② ③ ④ ⑤ ⑥ ⑦ ⑧ ⑨ ⑩

NOTES

....
....
....

WOULD YOU TRY AGAIN?   **OVERALL RATING**

☐ YES   ☐ NO   ⭐ ⭐ ⭐ ⭐ ⭐

Cigar Tasting Journal

NAME OF CIGAR

DATE   ORIGIN

BRAND   TYPE

WRAPPER   FILLER

SAMPLED   LENGTH / RING SIZE

PLACE CIGAR LABLE HERE

FLAVOR

- [ ] BITTER
- [ ] SPICY
- [ ] WOODY
- [ ] EARTHY
- [ ] NUTTY
- [ ] CREAMY
- [ ] CHOCOLATE
- [ ] TOFFEE
- [ ] SWEET
- [ ] FLORAL
- [ ] FRUITY
- [ ] SOUR
- [ ] HERBAL
- [ ] OILY
- [ ] LEATHER

FLAVOR STRENGTH

(1) (2) (3) (4) (5) (6) (7) (8) (9) (10)

NOTES

....
....
....

WOULD YOU TRY AGAIN?   **OVERALL RATING**

- [ ] YES   - [ ] NO   ★ ★ ★ ★ ★

Cigar Tasting Journal

NAME OF CIGAR

DATE   **ORIGIN**

BRAND   **TYPE**

WRAPPER   **FILLER**

SAMPLED   **LENGTH / RING SIZE**

PLACE CIGAR LABLE HERE

FLAVOR

- ☐ BITTER
- ☐ SPICY
- ☐ WOODY
- ☐ EARTHY
- ☐ NUTTY
- ☐ CREAMY
- ☐ CHOCOLATE
- ☐ TOFFEE
- ☐ SWEET
- ☐ FLORAL
- ☐ FRUITY
- ☐ SOUR
- ☐ HERBAL
- ☐ OILY
- ☐ LEATHER

FLAVOR STRENGTH

① ② ③ ④ ⑤ ⑥ ⑦ ⑧ ⑨ ⑩

NOTES

....
....
....

WOULD YOU TRY AGAIN?

☐ YES   ☐ NO

OVERALL RATING

★ ★ ★ ★ ★

Cigar Tasting Journal

NAME OF CIGAR

DATE   **ORIGIN**

BRAND   **TYPE**

WRAPPER   **FILLER**

SAMPLED   **LENGTH / RING SIZE**

PLACE CIGAR LABLE HERE

FLAVOR

☐ BITTER   ☐ CREAMY   ☐ FRUITY
☐ SPICY   ☐ CHOCOLATE   ☐ SOUR
☐ WOODY   ☐ TOFFEE   ☐ HERBAL
☐ EARTHY   ☐ SWEET   ☐ OILY
☐ NUTTY   ☐ FLORAL   ☐ LEATHER

FLAVOR STRENGTH

① ② ③ ④ ⑤ ⑥ ⑦ ⑧ ⑨ ⑩

NOTES

....
....
....

WOULD YOU TRY AGAIN?   **OVERALL RATING**

☐ YES   ☐ NO   ★ ★ ★ ★ ★

Cigar Tasting Journal

NAME OF CIGAR

DATE   **ORIGIN**

BRAND   **TYPE**

WRAPPER   **FILLER**

SAMPLED   **LENGTH / RING SIZE**

PLACE CIGAR LABLE HERE

FLAVOR

☐ BITTER   ☐ CREAMY   ☐ FRUITY
☐ SPICY   ☐ CHOCOLATE   ☐ SOUR
☐ WOODY   ☐ TOFFEE   ☐ HERBAL
☐ EARTHY   ☐ SWEET   ☐ OILY
☐ NUTTY   ☐ FLORAL   ☐ LEATHER

FLAVOR STRENGTH

① ② ③ ④ ⑤ ⑥ ⑦ ⑧ ⑨ ⑩

NOTES

....
....
....

WOULD YOU TRY AGAIN?   ## OVERALL RATING

☐ YES   ☐ NO   ★ ★ ★ ★ ★

Cigar Tasting Journal

NAME OF CIGAR

DATE   **ORIGIN**

BRAND   **TYPE**

WRAPPER   **FILLER**

SAMPLED   **LENGTH / RING SIZE**

PLACE CIGAR LABLE HERE

FLAVOR

- [ ] BITTER
- [ ] SPICY
- [ ] WOODY
- [ ] EARTHY
- [ ] NUTTY
- [ ] CREAMY
- [ ] CHOCOLATE
- [ ] TOFFEE
- [ ] SWEET
- [ ] FLORAL
- [ ] FRUITY
- [ ] SOUR
- [ ] HERBAL
- [ ] OILY
- [ ] LEATHER

FLAVOR STRENGTH

(1) (2) (3) (4) (5) (6) (7) (8) (9) (10)

NOTES

....
....
....

WOULD YOU TRY AGAIN?   **OVERALL RATING**

- [ ] YES   - [ ] NO   ★ ★ ★ ★ ★

Cigar Tasting Journal

NAME OF CIGAR

DATE   **ORIGIN**

BRAND   **TYPE**

WRAPPER   **FILLER**

SAMPLED   **LENGTH / RING SIZE**

PLACE CIGAR LABLE HERE

FLAVOR

- [ ] BITTER
- [ ] SPICY
- [ ] WOODY
- [ ] EARTHY
- [ ] NUTTY
- [ ] CREAMY
- [ ] CHOCOLATE
- [ ] TOFFEE
- [ ] SWEET
- [ ] FLORAL
- [ ] FRUITY
- [ ] SOUR
- [ ] HERBAL
- [ ] OILY
- [ ] LEATHER

FLAVOR STRENGTH

(1) (2) (3) (4) (5) (6) (7) (8) (9) (10)

NOTES

....
....
....

WOULD YOU TRY AGAIN?

- [ ] YES
- [ ] NO

OVERALL RATING

★ ★ ★ ★ ★

Cigar Tasting Journal

NAME OF CIGAR

DATE   **ORIGIN**

BRAND   **TYPE**

WRAPPER   **FILLER**

SAMPLED   **LENGTH / RING SIZE**

PLACE CIGAR LABLE HERE

FLAVOR

- [ ] BITTER
- [ ] SPICY
- [ ] WOODY
- [ ] EARTHY
- [ ] NUTTY

- [ ] CREAMY
- [ ] CHOCOLATE
- [ ] TOFFEE
- [ ] SWEET
- [ ] FLORAL

- [ ] FRUITY
- [ ] SOUR
- [ ] HERBAL
- [ ] OILY
- [ ] LEATHER

FLAVOR STRENGTH

(1) (2) (3) (4) (5) (6) (7) (8) (9) (10)

NOTES

....
....
....

WOULD YOU TRY AGAIN?

- [ ] YES   - [ ] NO

OVERALL RATING

★ ★ ★ ★ ★

Cigar Tasting Journal

NAME OF CIGAR

DATE   **ORIGIN**

BRAND   **TYPE**

WRAPPER   **FILLER**

SAMPLED   **LENGTH / RING SIZE**

PLACE CIGAR LABLE HERE

FLAVOR

- [ ] BITTER
- [ ] SPICY
- [ ] WOODY
- [ ] EARTHY
- [ ] NUTTY
- [ ] CREAMY
- [ ] CHOCOLATE
- [ ] TOFFEE
- [ ] SWEET
- [ ] FLORAL
- [ ] FRUITY
- [ ] SOUR
- [ ] HERBAL
- [ ] OILY
- [ ] LEATHER

FLAVOR STRENGTH

① ② ③ ④ ⑤ ⑥ ⑦ ⑧ ⑨ ⑩

NOTES

....
....
....

WOULD YOU TRY AGAIN?

- [ ] YES   - [ ] NO

OVERALL RATING

★ ★ ★ ★ ★

Cigar Tasting Journal

NAME OF CIGAR

DATE

ORIGIN

BRAND

TYPE

WRAPPER

FILLER

SAMPLED

LENGTH / RING SIZE

PLACE CIGAR LABLE HERE

FLAVOR

☐ BITTER
☐ SPICY
☐ WOODY
☐ EARTHY
☐ NUTTY

☐ CREAMY
☐ CHOCOLATE
☐ TOFFEE
☐ SWEET
☐ FLORAL

☐ FRUITY
☐ SOUR
☐ HERBAL
☐ OILY
☐ LEATHER

FLAVOR STRENGTH

① ② ③ ④ ⑤ ⑥ ⑦ ⑧ ⑨ ⑩

NOTES

....
....
....

WOULD YOU TRY AGAIN?

☐ YES   ☐ NO

OVERALL RATING

★ ★ ★ ★ ★

Cigar Tasting Journal

NAME OF CIGAR

DATE   **ORIGIN**

BRAND   **TYPE**

WRAPPER   **FILLER**

SAMPLED   **LENGTH / RING SIZE**

PLACE CIGAR LABLE HERE

FLAVOR

- [ ] BITTER
- [ ] SPICY
- [ ] WOODY
- [ ] EARTHY
- [ ] NUTTY
- [ ] CREAMY
- [ ] CHOCOLATE
- [ ] TOFFEE
- [ ] SWEET
- [ ] FLORAL
- [ ] FRUITY
- [ ] SOUR
- [ ] HERBAL
- [ ] OILY
- [ ] LEATHER

FLAVOR STRENGTH

(1) (2) (3) (4) (5) (6) (7) (8) (9) (10)

NOTES

....
....
....

WOULD YOU TRY AGAIN?

- [ ] YES
- [ ] NO

OVERALL RATING

★ ★ ★ ★ ★

Cigar Tasting Journal

NAME OF CIGAR

DATE | **ORIGIN**

BRAND | **TYPE**

WRAPPER | **FILLER**

SAMPLED | **LENGTH / RING SIZE**

PLACE CIGAR LABLE HERE

FLAVOR

☐ BITTER ☐ CREAMY ☐ FRUITY
☐ SPICY ☐ CHOCOLATE ☐ SOUR
☐ WOODY ☐ TOFFEE ☐ HERBAL
☐ EARTHY ☐ SWEET ☐ OILY
☐ NUTTY ☐ FLORAL ☐ LEATHER

FLAVOR STRENGTH

① ② ③ ④ ⑤ ⑥ ⑦ ⑧ ⑨ ⑩

NOTES

....
....
....

WOULD YOU TRY AGAIN?

☐ YES ☐ NO

OVERALL RATING

★ ★ ★ ★ ★

Cigar Tasting Journal

NAME OF CIGAR

DATE   **ORIGIN**

BRAND   **TYPE**

WRAPPER   **FILLER**

SAMPLED   **LENGTH / RING SIZE**

PLACE CIGAR LABLE HERE

FLAVOR

- [ ] BITTER
- [ ] SPICY
- [ ] WOODY
- [ ] EARTHY
- [ ] NUTTY
- [ ] CREAMY
- [ ] CHOCOLATE
- [ ] TOFFEE
- [ ] SWEET
- [ ] FLORAL
- [ ] FRUITY
- [ ] SOUR
- [ ] HERBAL
- [ ] OILY
- [ ] LEATHER

FLAVOR STRENGTH

(1) (2) (3) (4) (5) (6) (7) (8) (9) (10)

NOTES

....
....
....

WOULD YOU TRY AGAIN?

- [ ] YES
- [ ] NO

OVERALL RATING

★ ★ ★ ★ ★

Cigar Tasting Journal

NAME OF CIGAR

DATE   **ORIGIN**

BRAND   **TYPE**

WRAPPER   **FILLER**

SAMPLED   **LENGTH / RING SIZE**

PLACE CIGAR LABLE HERE

FLAVOR

- ☐ BITTER
- ☐ SPICY
- ☐ WOODY
- ☐ EARTHY
- ☐ NUTTY

- ☐ CREAMY
- ☐ CHOCOLATE
- ☐ TOFFEE
- ☐ SWEET
- ☐ FLORAL

- ☐ FRUITY
- ☐ SOUR
- ☐ HERBAL
- ☐ OILY
- ☐ LEATHER

FLAVOR STRENGTH

① ② ③ ④ ⑤ ⑥ ⑦ ⑧ ⑨ ⑩

NOTES

....
....
....

WOULD YOU TRY AGAIN?

☐ YES   ☐ NO

OVERALL RATING

★ ★ ★ ★ ★

Cigar Tasting Journal

NAME OF CIGAR

DATE **ORIGIN**

BRAND **TYPE**

WRAPPER **FILLER**

SAMPLED **LENGTH / RING SIZE**

PLACE CIGAR LABLE HERE

FLAVOR

☐ BITTER ☐ CREAMY ☐ FRUITY
☐ SPICY ☐ CHOCOLATE ☐ SOUR
☐ WOODY ☐ TOFFEE ☐ HERBAL
☐ EARTHY ☐ SWEET ☐ OILY
☐ NUTTY ☐ FLORAL ☐ LEATHER

FLAVOR STRENGTH

① ② ③ ④ ⑤ ⑥ ⑦ ⑧ ⑨ ⑩

NOTES

....
....
....

WOULD YOU TRY AGAIN? **OVERALL RATING**

☐ YES ☐ NO ★ ★ ★ ★ ★

Cigar Tasting Journal

NAME OF CIGAR

DATE   **ORIGIN**

BRAND   **TYPE**

WRAPPER   **FILLER**

SAMPLED   **LENGTH / RING SIZE**

PLACE CIGAR LABLE HERE

FLAVOR

- [ ] BITTER
- [ ] SPICY
- [ ] WOODY
- [ ] EARTHY
- [ ] NUTTY
- [ ] CREAMY
- [ ] CHOCOLATE
- [ ] TOFFEE
- [ ] SWEET
- [ ] FLORAL
- [ ] FRUITY
- [ ] SOUR
- [ ] HERBAL
- [ ] OILY
- [ ] LEATHER

FLAVOR STRENGTH

(1) (2) (3) (4) (5) (6) (7) (8) (9) (10)

NOTES

....
....
....

WOULD YOU TRY AGAIN?

- [ ] YES
- [ ] NO

OVERALL RATING

★ ★ ★ ★ ★

Cigar Tasting Journal

NAME OF CIGAR

DATE   ORIGIN

BRAND   TYPE

WRAPPER   FILLER

SAMPLED   LENGTH / RING SIZE

PLACE CIGAR LABLE HERE

FLAVOR

- [ ] BITTER
- [ ] SPICY
- [ ] WOODY
- [ ] EARTHY
- [ ] NUTTY
- [ ] CREAMY
- [ ] CHOCOLATE
- [ ] TOFFEE
- [ ] SWEET
- [ ] FLORAL
- [ ] FRUITY
- [ ] SOUR
- [ ] HERBAL
- [ ] OILY
- [ ] LEATHER

FLAVOR STRENGTH

① ② ③ ④ ⑤ ⑥ ⑦ ⑧ ⑨ ⑩

NOTES

....
....
....

WOULD YOU TRY AGAIN?

- [ ] YES
- [ ] NO

OVERALL RATING

⭐ ⭐ ⭐ ⭐ ⭐

Cigar Tasting Journal

NAME OF CIGAR

DATE   **ORIGIN**

BRAND   **TYPE**

WRAPPER   **FILLER**

SAMPLED   **LENGTH / RING SIZE**

PLACE CIGAR LABLE HERE

FLAVOR

- [ ] BITTER
- [ ] SPICY
- [ ] WOODY
- [ ] EARTHY
- [ ] NUTTY

- [ ] CREAMY
- [ ] CHOCOLATE
- [ ] TOFFEE
- [ ] SWEET
- [ ] FLORAL

- [ ] FRUITY
- [ ] SOUR
- [ ] HERBAL
- [ ] OILY
- [ ] LEATHER

FLAVOR STRENGTH

(1) (2) (3) (4) (5) (6) (7) (8) (9) (10)

NOTES

WOULD YOU TRY AGAIN?

- [ ] YES
- [ ] NO

OVERALL RATING

★ ★ ★ ★ ★

Cigar Tasting Journal

NAME OF CIGAR

DATE   **ORIGIN**

BRAND   **TYPE**

WRAPPER   **FILLER**

SAMPLED   **LENGTH / RING SIZE**

PLACE CIGAR LABLE HERE

FLAVOR

☐ BITTER   ☐ CREAMY   ☐ FRUITY
☐ SPICY   ☐ CHOCOLATE   ☐ SOUR
☐ WOODY   ☐ TOFFEE   ☐ HERBAL
☐ EARTHY   ☐ SWEET   ☐ OILY
☐ NUTTY   ☐ FLORAL   ☐ LEATHER

FLAVOR STRENGTH

① ② ③ ④ ⑤ ⑥ ⑦ ⑧ ⑨ ⑩

NOTES

....
....
....

WOULD YOU TRY AGAIN?   **OVERALL RATING**

☐ YES   ☐ NO   ★ ★ ★ ★ ★

Cigar Tasting Journal

NAME OF CIGAR

DATE   **ORIGIN**

BRAND   **TYPE**

WRAPPER   **FILLER**

SAMPLED   **LENGTH / RING SIZE**

PLACE CIGAR LABLE HERE

FLAVOR

- ☐ BITTER
- ☐ SPICY
- ☐ WOODY
- ☐ EARTHY
- ☐ NUTTY

- ☐ CREAMY
- ☐ CHOCOLATE
- ☐ TOFFEE
- ☐ SWEET
- ☐ FLORAL

- ☐ FRUITY
- ☐ SOUR
- ☐ HERBAL
- ☐ OILY
- ☐ LEATHER

FLAVOR STRENGTH

① ② ③ ④ ⑤ ⑥ ⑦ ⑧ ⑨ ⑩

NOTES

....
....
....

WOULD YOU TRY AGAIN?

☐ YES   ☐ NO

OVERALL RATING

★ ★ ★ ★ ★

Cigar Tasting Journal

NAME OF CIGAR

DATE   ORIGIN

BRAND   TYPE

WRAPPER   FILLER

SAMPLED   LENGTH / RING SIZE

PLACE CIGAR LABLE HERE

FLAVOR

- ☐ BITTER
- ☐ SPICY
- ☐ WOODY
- ☐ EARTHY
- ☐ NUTTY
- ☐ CREAMY
- ☐ CHOCOLATE
- ☐ TOFFEE
- ☐ SWEET
- ☐ FLORAL
- ☐ FRUITY
- ☐ SOUR
- ☐ HERBAL
- ☐ OILY
- ☐ LEATHER

FLAVOR STRENGTH

① ② ③ ④ ⑤ ⑥ ⑦ ⑧ ⑨ ⑩

NOTES

....
....
....

WOULD YOU TRY AGAIN?

☐ YES   ☐ NO

OVERALL RATING

★ ★ ★ ★ ★

Cigar Tasting Journal

NAME OF CIGAR

DATE   **ORIGIN**

BRAND   **TYPE**

WRAPPER   **FILLER**

SAMPLED   **LENGTH / RING SIZE**

PLACE CIGAR LABLE HERE

FLAVOR

- ☐ BITTER
- ☐ SPICY
- ☐ WOODY
- ☐ EARTHY
- ☐ NUTTY
- ☐ CREAMY
- ☐ CHOCOLATE
- ☐ TOFFEE
- ☐ SWEET
- ☐ FLORAL
- ☐ FRUITY
- ☐ SOUR
- ☐ HERBAL
- ☐ OILY
- ☐ LEATHER

FLAVOR STRENGTH

① ② ③ ④ ⑤ ⑥ ⑦ ⑧ ⑨ ⑩

NOTES

....
....
....

WOULD YOU TRY AGAIN?

☐ YES   ☐ NO

OVERALL RATING

★ ★ ★ ★ ★

Cigar Tasting Journal

NAME OF CIGAR

DATE   **ORIGIN**

BRAND   **TYPE**

WRAPPER   **FILLER**

SAMPLED   **LENGTH / RING SIZE**

PLACE CIGAR LABLE HERE

FLAVOR

- [ ] BITTER
- [ ] SPICY
- [ ] WOODY
- [ ] EARTHY
- [ ] NUTTY
- [ ] CREAMY
- [ ] CHOCOLATE
- [ ] TOFFEE
- [ ] SWEET
- [ ] FLORAL
- [ ] FRUITY
- [ ] SOUR
- [ ] HERBAL
- [ ] OILY
- [ ] LEATHER

FLAVOR STRENGTH

(1) (2) (3) (4) (5) (6) (7) (8) (9) (10)

NOTES

....
....
....

WOULD YOU TRY AGAIN?   **OVERALL RATING**

- [ ] YES   - [ ] NO   ★ ★ ★ ★ ★

Cigar Tasting Journal

NAME OF CIGAR

DATE   **ORIGIN**

BRAND   **TYPE**

WRAPPER   **FILLER**

SAMPLED   **LENGTH / RING SIZE**

PLACE CIGAR LABLE HERE

FLAVOR

- [ ] BITTER
- [ ] SPICY
- [ ] WOODY
- [ ] EARTHY
- [ ] NUTTY
- [ ] CREAMY
- [ ] CHOCOLATE
- [ ] TOFFEE
- [ ] SWEET
- [ ] FLORAL
- [ ] FRUITY
- [ ] SOUR
- [ ] HERBAL
- [ ] OILY
- [ ] LEATHER

FLAVOR STRENGTH

(1) (2) (3) (4) (5) (6) (7) (8) (9) (10)

NOTES

....
....
....

WOULD YOU TRY AGAIN?

- [ ] YES
- [ ] NO

OVERALL RATING

★ ★ ★ ★ ★

Cigar Tasting Journal

NAME OF CIGAR

DATE　　　　　　　　　　　**ORIGIN**

BRAND　　　　　　　　　　　**TYPE**

WRAPPER　　　　　　　　　**FILLER**

SAMPLED　　　　　　　　　**LENGTH / RING SIZE**

PLACE CIGAR LABLE HERE

FLAVOR

☐ BITTER　　☐ CREAMY　　☐ FRUITY

☐ SPICY　　☐ CHOCOLATE　　☐ SOUR

☐ WOODY　　☐ TOFFEE　　☐ HERBAL

☐ EARTHY　　☐ SWEET　　☐ OILY

☐ NUTTY　　☐ FLORAL　　☐ LEATHER

FLAVOR STRENGTH

① ② ③ ④ ⑤ ⑥ ⑦ ⑧ ⑨ ⑩

NOTES

....
....
....

WOULD YOU TRY AGAIN?　　　　**OVERALL RATING**

☐ YES　　　☐ NO　　　　★ ★ ★ ★ ★

Cigar Tasting Journal

NAME OF CIGAR

DATE   **ORIGIN**

BRAND   **TYPE**

WRAPPER   **FILLER**

SAMPLED   **LENGTH / RING SIZE**

PLACE CIGAR LABLE HERE

FLAVOR

- ☐ BITTER
- ☐ SPICY
- ☐ WOODY
- ☐ EARTHY
- ☐ NUTTY

- ☐ CREAMY
- ☐ CHOCOLATE
- ☐ TOFFEE
- ☐ SWEET
- ☐ FLORAL

- ☐ FRUITY
- ☐ SOUR
- ☐ HERBAL
- ☐ OILY
- ☐ LEATHER

FLAVOR STRENGTH

① ② ③ ④ ⑤ ⑥ ⑦ ⑧ ⑨ ⑩

NOTES

....
....
....

WOULD YOU TRY AGAIN?

☐ YES   ☐ NO

OVERALL RATING

★ ★ ★ ★ ★

Cigar Tasting Journal

NAME OF CIGAR

DATE   **ORIGIN**

BRAND   **TYPE**

WRAPPER   **FILLER**

SAMPLED   **LENGTH / RING SIZE**

PLACE CIGAR LABLE HERE

FLAVOR

☐ BITTER   ☐ CREAMY   ☐ FRUITY
☐ SPICY   ☐ CHOCOLATE   ☐ SOUR
☐ WOODY   ☐ TOFFEE   ☐ HERBAL
☐ EARTHY   ☐ SWEET   ☐ OILY
☐ NUTTY   ☐ FLORAL   ☐ LEATHER

FLAVOR STRENGTH

① ② ③ ④ ⑤ ⑥ ⑦ ⑧ ⑨ ⑩

NOTES

....
....
....

WOULD YOU TRY AGAIN?   **OVERALL RATING**

☐ YES   ☐ NO   ★ ★ ★ ★ ★

Cigar Tasting Journal

NAME OF CIGAR

DATE　　　　　　　　　　　　　**ORIGIN**

BRAND　　　　　　　　　　　　**TYPE**

WRAPPER　　　　　　　　　　　**FILLER**

SAMPLED　　　　　　　　　　　**LENGTH / RING SIZE**

PLACE CIGAR LABLE HERE

FLAVOR

- [ ] BITTER
- [ ] SPICY
- [ ] WOODY
- [ ] EARTHY
- [ ] NUTTY
- [ ] CREAMY
- [ ] CHOCOLATE
- [ ] TOFFEE
- [ ] SWEET
- [ ] FLORAL
- [ ] FRUITY
- [ ] SOUR
- [ ] HERBAL
- [ ] OILY
- [ ] LEATHER

FLAVOR STRENGTH

(1) (2) (3) (4) (5) (6) (7) (8) (9) (10)

NOTES

....
....
....

WOULD YOU TRY AGAIN?　　　　**OVERALL RATING**

- [ ] YES
- [ ] NO

★ ★ ★ ★ ★

Cigar Tasting Journal

NAME OF CIGAR

DATE   **ORIGIN**

BRAND   **TYPE**

WRAPPER   **FILLER**

SAMPLED   **LENGTH / RING SIZE**

PLACE CIGAR LABLE HERE

FLAVOR

- ☐ BITTER
- ☐ SPICY
- ☐ WOODY
- ☐ EARTHY
- ☐ NUTTY
- ☐ CREAMY
- ☐ CHOCOLATE
- ☐ TOFFEE
- ☐ SWEET
- ☐ FLORAL
- ☐ FRUITY
- ☐ SOUR
- ☐ HERBAL
- ☐ OILY
- ☐ LEATHER

FLAVOR STRENGTH

① ② ③ ④ ⑤ ⑥ ⑦ ⑧ ⑨ ⑩

NOTES

....
....
....

WOULD YOU TRY AGAIN?   **OVERALL RATING**

☐ YES   ☐ NO   ★ ★ ★ ★ ★

Cigar Tasting Journal

NAME OF CIGAR

DATE   **ORIGIN**

BRAND   **TYPE**

WRAPPER   **FILLER**

SAMPLED   **LENGTH / RING SIZE**

PLACE CIGAR LABLE HERE

FLAVOR

- ☐ BITTER
- ☐ SPICY
- ☐ WOODY
- ☐ EARTHY
- ☐ NUTTY
- ☐ CREAMY
- ☐ CHOCOLATE
- ☐ TOFFEE
- ☐ SWEET
- ☐ FLORAL
- ☐ FRUITY
- ☐ SOUR
- ☐ HERBAL
- ☐ OILY
- ☐ LEATHER

FLAVOR STRENGTH

① ② ③ ④ ⑤ ⑥ ⑦ ⑧ ⑨ ⑩

NOTES

....
....
....

WOULD YOU TRY AGAIN?   **OVERALL RATING**

☐ YES   ☐ NO   ★ ★ ★ ★ ★

Cigar Tasting Journal

NAME OF CIGAR

DATE **ORIGIN**

BRAND **TYPE**

WRAPPER **FILLER**

SAMPLED **LENGTH / RING SIZE**

PLACE CIGAR LABLE HERE

FLAVOR

- [ ] BITTER
- [ ] SPICY
- [ ] WOODY
- [ ] EARTHY
- [ ] NUTTY
- [ ] CREAMY
- [ ] CHOCOLATE
- [ ] TOFFEE
- [ ] SWEET
- [ ] FLORAL
- [ ] FRUITY
- [ ] SOUR
- [ ] HERBAL
- [ ] OILY
- [ ] LEATHER

FLAVOR STRENGTH

(1) (2) (3) (4) (5) (6) (7) (8) (9) (10)

NOTES

....
....
....

WOULD YOU TRY AGAIN?

- [ ] YES
- [ ] NO

OVERALL RATING

★ ★ ★ ★ ★

Cigar Tasting Journal

NAME OF CIGAR

DATE   **ORIGIN**

BRAND   **TYPE**

WRAPPER   **FILLER**

SAMPLED   **LENGTH / RING SIZE**

PLACE CIGAR LABLE HERE

FLAVOR

- [ ] BITTER
- [ ] SPICY
- [ ] WOODY
- [ ] EARTHY
- [ ] NUTTY
- [ ] CREAMY
- [ ] CHOCOLATE
- [ ] TOFFEE
- [ ] SWEET
- [ ] FLORAL
- [ ] FRUITY
- [ ] SOUR
- [ ] HERBAL
- [ ] OILY
- [ ] LEATHER

FLAVOR STRENGTH

(1) (2) (3) (4) (5) (6) (7) (8) (9) (10)

NOTES

....
....
....

WOULD YOU TRY AGAIN?   **OVERALL RATING**

- [ ] YES   - [ ] NO   ★ ★ ★ ★ ★

Cigar Tasting Journal

NAME OF CIGAR

DATE　　　　　　　　　　　**ORIGIN**

BRAND　　　　　　　　　　**TYPE**

WRAPPER　　　　　　　　**FILLER**

SAMPLED　　　　　　　　**LENGTH / RING SIZE**

PLACE CIGAR LABLE HERE

FLAVOR

- ☐ BITTER
- ☐ SPICY
- ☐ WOODY
- ☐ EARTHY
- ☐ NUTTY

- ☐ CREAMY
- ☐ CHOCOLATE
- ☐ TOFFEE
- ☐ SWEET
- ☐ FLORAL

- ☐ FRUITY
- ☐ SOUR
- ☐ HERBAL
- ☐ OILY
- ☐ LEATHER

FLAVOR STRENGTH

① ② ③ ④ ⑤ ⑥ ⑦ ⑧ ⑨ ⑩

NOTES

....
....
....

WOULD YOU TRY AGAIN?

☐ YES　　☐ NO

OVERALL RATING

★ ★ ★ ★ ★

Cigar Tasting Journal

NAME OF CIGAR

DATE | **ORIGIN**

BRAND | **TYPE**

WRAPPER | **FILLER**

SAMPLED | **LENGTH / RING SIZE**

PLACE CIGAR LABLE HERE

FLAVOR

- [ ] BITTER
- [ ] SPICY
- [ ] WOODY
- [ ] EARTHY
- [ ] NUTTY
- [ ] CREAMY
- [ ] CHOCOLATE
- [ ] TOFFEE
- [ ] SWEET
- [ ] FLORAL
- [ ] FRUITY
- [ ] SOUR
- [ ] HERBAL
- [ ] OILY
- [ ] LEATHER

FLAVOR STRENGTH

① ② ③ ④ ⑤ ⑥ ⑦ ⑧ ⑨ ⑩

NOTES

....
....
....

WOULD YOU TRY AGAIN?

- [ ] YES
- [ ] NO

OVERALL RATING

★ ★ ★ ★ ★

Cigar Tasting Journal

NAME OF CIGAR

DATE   ORIGIN

BRAND   TYPE

WRAPPER   FILLER

SAMPLED   LENGTH / RING SIZE

PLACE CIGAR LABLE HERE

FLAVOR

- [ ] BITTER
- [ ] SPICY
- [ ] WOODY
- [ ] EARTHY
- [ ] NUTTY
- [ ] CREAMY
- [ ] CHOCOLATE
- [ ] TOFFEE
- [ ] SWEET
- [ ] FLORAL
- [ ] FRUITY
- [ ] SOUR
- [ ] HERBAL
- [ ] OILY
- [ ] LEATHER

FLAVOR STRENGTH

(1) (2) (3) (4) (5) (6) (7) (8) (9) (10)

NOTES

....
....
....

WOULD YOU TRY AGAIN?   **OVERALL RATING**

- [ ] YES   - [ ] NO   ☆ ☆ ☆ ☆ ☆

Cigar Tasting Journal

NAME OF CIGAR

DATE   **ORIGIN**

BRAND   **TYPE**

WRAPPER   **FILLER**

SAMPLED   **LENGTH / RING SIZE**

PLACE CIGAR LABLE HERE

FLAVOR

- ☐ BITTER
- ☐ SPICY
- ☐ WOODY
- ☐ EARTHY
- ☐ NUTTY

- ☐ CREAMY
- ☐ CHOCOLATE
- ☐ TOFFEE
- ☐ SWEET
- ☐ FLORAL

- ☐ FRUITY
- ☐ SOUR
- ☐ HERBAL
- ☐ OILY
- ☐ LEATHER

FLAVOR STRENGTH

① ② ③ ④ ⑤ ⑥ ⑦ ⑧ ⑨ ⑩

NOTES

....
....
....

WOULD YOU TRY AGAIN?   **OVERALL RATING**

☐ YES   ☐ NO   ★ ★ ★ ★ ★

Cigar Tasting Journal

NAME OF CIGAR

DATE   **ORIGIN**

BRAND   **TYPE**

WRAPPER   **FILLER**

SAMPLED   **LENGTH / RING SIZE**

> PLACE CIGAR LABLE HERE

FLAVOR

- ☐ BITTER
- ☐ SPICY
- ☐ WOODY
- ☐ EARTHY
- ☐ NUTTY
- ☐ CREAMY
- ☐ CHOCOLATE
- ☐ TOFFEE
- ☐ SWEET
- ☐ FLORAL
- ☐ FRUITY
- ☐ SOUR
- ☐ HERBAL
- ☐ OILY
- ☐ LEATHER

FLAVOR STRENGTH

① ② ③ ④ ⑤ ⑥ ⑦ ⑧ ⑨ ⑩

NOTES

....
....
....

WOULD YOU TRY AGAIN?

☐ YES   ☐ NO

OVERALL RATING

★ ★ ★ ★ ★

Cigar Tasting Journal

NAME OF CIGAR

DATE   **ORIGIN**

BRAND   **TYPE**

WRAPPER   **FILLER**

SAMPLED   **LENGTH / RING SIZE**

PLACE CIGAR LABLE HERE

FLAVOR

- [ ] BITTER
- [ ] SPICY
- [ ] WOODY
- [ ] EARTHY
- [ ] NUTTY

- [ ] CREAMY
- [ ] CHOCOLATE
- [ ] TOFFEE
- [ ] SWEET
- [ ] FLORAL

- [ ] FRUITY
- [ ] SOUR
- [ ] HERBAL
- [ ] OILY
- [ ] LEATHER

FLAVOR STRENGTH

(1) (2) (3) (4) (5) (6) (7) (8) (9) (10)

NOTES

....
....
....

WOULD YOU TRY AGAIN?   **OVERALL RATING**

- [ ] YES   - [ ] NO   ★ ★ ★ ★ ★

Cigar Tasting Journal

NAME OF CIGAR

DATE   ORIGIN

BRAND   TYPE

WRAPPER   FILLER

SAMPLED   LENGTH / RING SIZE

PLACE CIGAR LABLE HERE

FLAVOR

☐ BITTER   ☐ CREAMY   ☐ FRUITY
☐ SPICY   ☐ CHOCOLATE   ☐ SOUR
☐ WOODY   ☐ TOFFEE   ☐ HERBAL
☐ EARTHY   ☐ SWEET   ☐ OILY
☐ NUTTY   ☐ FLORAL   ☐ LEATHER

FLAVOR STRENGTH

① ② ③ ④ ⑤ ⑥ ⑦ ⑧ ⑨ ⑩

NOTES

....
....
....

WOULD YOU TRY AGAIN?   **OVERALL RATING**

☐ YES   ☐ NO   ★ ★ ★ ★ ★

Cigar Tasting Journal

NAME OF CIGAR

DATE

BRAND

WRAPPER

SAMPLED

ORIGIN

TYPE

FILLER

LENGTH / RING SIZE

PLACE CIGAR LABLE HERE

FLAVOR

- [ ] BITTER
- [ ] SPICY
- [ ] WOODY
- [ ] EARTHY
- [ ] NUTTY

- [ ] CREAMY
- [ ] CHOCOLATE
- [ ] TOFFEE
- [ ] SWEET
- [ ] FLORAL

- [ ] FRUITY
- [ ] SOUR
- [ ] HERBAL
- [ ] OILY
- [ ] LEATHER

FLAVOR STRENGTH

(1) (2) (3) (4) (5) (6) (7) (8) (9) (10)

NOTES

....
....
....

WOULD YOU TRY AGAIN?

- [ ] YES
- [ ] NO

OVERALL RATING

★ ★ ★ ★ ★

Cigar Tasting Journal

NAME OF CIGAR

DATE   **ORIGIN**

BRAND   **TYPE**

WRAPPER   **FILLER**

SAMPLED   **LENGTH / RING SIZE**

PLACE CIGAR LABLE HERE

FLAVOR

☐ BITTER   ☐ CREAMY   ☐ FRUITY
☐ SPICY   ☐ CHOCOLATE   ☐ SOUR
☐ WOODY   ☐ TOFFEE   ☐ HERBAL
☐ EARTHY   ☐ SWEET   ☐ OILY
☐ NUTTY   ☐ FLORAL   ☐ LEATHER

FLAVOR STRENGTH

① ② ③ ④ ⑤ ⑥ ⑦ ⑧ ⑨ ⑩

NOTES

....
....
....

WOULD YOU TRY AGAIN?   **OVERALL RATING**

☐ YES   ☐ NO   ★ ★ ★ ★ ★

Cigar Tasting Journal

NAME OF CIGAR

DATE   **ORIGIN**

BRAND   **TYPE**

WRAPPER   **FILLER**

SAMPLED   **LENGTH / RING SIZE**

PLACE CIGAR LABLE HERE

FLAVOR

- [ ] BITTER
- [ ] SPICY
- [ ] WOODY
- [ ] EARTHY
- [ ] NUTTY

- [ ] CREAMY
- [ ] CHOCOLATE
- [ ] TOFFEE
- [ ] SWEET
- [ ] FLORAL

- [ ] FRUITY
- [ ] SOUR
- [ ] HERBAL
- [ ] OILY
- [ ] LEATHER

FLAVOR STRENGTH

(1) (2) (3) (4) (5) (6) (7) (8) (9) (10)

NOTES

....
....
....

WOULD YOU TRY AGAIN?

- [ ] YES
- [ ] NO

OVERALL RATING

⭐ ⭐ ⭐ ⭐ ⭐

Cigar Tasting Journal

NAME OF CIGAR

DATE   **ORIGIN**

BRAND   **TYPE**

WRAPPER   **FILLER**

SAMPLED   **LENGTH / RING SIZE**

PLACE CIGAR LABLE HERE

FLAVOR

☐ BITTER   ☐ CREAMY   ☐ FRUITY
☐ SPICY   ☐ CHOCOLATE   ☐ SOUR
☐ WOODY   ☐ TOFFEE   ☐ HERBAL
☐ EARTHY   ☐ SWEET   ☐ OILY
☐ NUTTY   ☐ FLORAL   ☐ LEATHER

FLAVOR STRENGTH

① ② ③ ④ ⑤ ⑥ ⑦ ⑧ ⑨ ⑩

NOTES

....
....
....

WOULD YOU TRY AGAIN?

☐ YES   ☐ NO

OVERALL RATING

★ ★ ★ ★ ★

Cigar Tasting Journal

NAME OF CIGAR

DATE   **ORIGIN**

BRAND   **TYPE**

WRAPPER   **FILLER**

SAMPLED   **LENGTH / RING SIZE**

PLACE CIGAR LABLE HERE

FLAVOR

- ☐ BITTER
- ☐ SPICY
- ☐ WOODY
- ☐ EARTHY
- ☐ NUTTY
- ☐ CREAMY
- ☐ CHOCOLATE
- ☐ TOFFEE
- ☐ SWEET
- ☐ FLORAL
- ☐ FRUITY
- ☐ SOUR
- ☐ HERBAL
- ☐ OILY
- ☐ LEATHER

FLAVOR STRENGTH

① ② ③ ④ ⑤ ⑥ ⑦ ⑧ ⑨ ⑩

NOTES

....
....
....

WOULD YOU TRY AGAIN?   **OVERALL RATING**

☐ YES   ☐ NO   ★ ★ ★ ★ ★

Cigar Tasting Journal

NAME OF CIGAR

DATE   **ORIGIN**

BRAND   **TYPE**

WRAPPER   **FILLER**

SAMPLED   **LENGTH / RING SIZE**

PLACE CIGAR LABLE HERE

FLAVOR

☐ BITTER   ☐ CREAMY   ☐ FRUITY

☐ SPICY   ☐ CHOCOLATE   ☐ SOUR

☐ WOODY   ☐ TOFFEE   ☐ HERBAL

☐ EARTHY   ☐ SWEET   ☐ OILY

☐ NUTTY   ☐ FLORAL   ☐ LEATHER

FLAVOR STRENGTH

① ② ③ ④ ⑤ ⑥ ⑦ ⑧ ⑨ ⑩

NOTES

....

....

....

WOULD YOU TRY AGAIN?   **OVERALL RATING**

☐ YES   ☐ NO   ★ ★ ★ ★ ★

Cigar Tasting Journal

NAME OF CIGAR

DATE   **ORIGIN**

BRAND   **TYPE**

WRAPPER   **FILLER**

SAMPLED   **LENGTH / RING SIZE**

PLACE CIGAR LABLE HERE

FLAVOR

- [ ] BITTER
- [ ] SPICY
- [ ] WOODY
- [ ] EARTHY
- [ ] NUTTY
- [ ] CREAMY
- [ ] CHOCOLATE
- [ ] TOFFEE
- [ ] SWEET
- [ ] FLORAL
- [ ] FRUITY
- [ ] SOUR
- [ ] HERBAL
- [ ] OILY
- [ ] LEATHER

FLAVOR STRENGTH

(1) (2) (3) (4) (5) (6) (7) (8) (9) (10)

NOTES

....
....
....

WOULD YOU TRY AGAIN?   **OVERALL RATING**

- [ ] YES   - [ ] NO   ★ ★ ★ ★ ★

Cigar Tasting Journal

NAME OF CIGAR

DATE   ORIGIN

BRAND   TYPE

WRAPPER   FILLER

SAMPLED   LENGTH / RING SIZE

PLACE CIGAR LABLE HERE

FLAVOR

☐ BITTER   ☐ CREAMY   ☐ FRUITY
☐ SPICY   ☐ CHOCOLATE   ☐ SOUR
☐ WOODY   ☐ TOFFEE   ☐ HERBAL
☐ EARTHY   ☐ SWEET   ☐ OILY
☐ NUTTY   ☐ FLORAL   ☐ LEATHER

FLAVOR STRENGTH

① ② ③ ④ ⑤ ⑥ ⑦ ⑧ ⑨ ⑩

NOTES

....
....
....

WOULD YOU TRY AGAIN?   **OVERALL RATING**

☐ YES   ☐ NO   ⭐ ⭐ ⭐ ⭐ ⭐

Cigar Tasting Journal

NAME OF CIGAR

DATE

ORIGIN

BRAND

TYPE

WRAPPER

FILLER

SAMPLED

LENGTH / RING SIZE

PLACE CIGAR LABLE HERE

FLAVOR

- ☐ BITTER
- ☐ SPICY
- ☐ WOODY
- ☐ EARTHY
- ☐ NUTTY
- ☐ CREAMY
- ☐ CHOCOLATE
- ☐ TOFFEE
- ☐ SWEET
- ☐ FLORAL
- ☐ FRUITY
- ☐ SOUR
- ☐ HERBAL
- ☐ OILY
- ☐ LEATHER

FLAVOR STRENGTH

① ② ③ ④ ⑤ ⑥ ⑦ ⑧ ⑨ ⑩

NOTES

....
....
....

WOULD YOU TRY AGAIN?

☐ YES   ☐ NO

OVERALL RATING

★ ★ ★ ★ ★

Cigar Tasting Journal

NAME OF CIGAR

DATE　　　　　　　　　　**ORIGIN**

BRAND　　　　　　　　　　**TYPE**

WRAPPER　　　　　　　　**FILLER**

SAMPLED　　　　　　　　**LENGTH / RING SIZE**

PLACE CIGAR LABLE HERE

FLAVOR

☐ BITTER ☐ CREAMY ☐ FRUITY
☐ SPICY ☐ CHOCOLATE ☐ SOUR
☐ WOODY ☐ TOFFEE ☐ HERBAL
☐ EARTHY ☐ SWEET ☐ OILY
☐ NUTTY ☐ FLORAL ☐ LEATHER

FLAVOR STRENGTH

①　②　③　④　⑤　⑥　⑦　⑧　⑨　⑩

NOTES

WOULD YOU TRY AGAIN?

☐ YES　　☐ NO

OVERALL RATING

★ ★ ★ ★ ★

Cigar Tasting Journal

NAME OF CIGAR

DATE **ORIGIN**

BRAND **TYPE**

WRAPPER **FILLER**

SAMPLED **LENGTH / RING SIZE**

PLACE CIGAR LABLE HERE

FLAVOR

- [ ] BITTER
- [ ] SPICY
- [ ] WOODY
- [ ] EARTHY
- [ ] NUTTY

- [ ] CREAMY
- [ ] CHOCOLATE
- [ ] TOFFEE
- [ ] SWEET
- [ ] FLORAL

- [ ] FRUITY
- [ ] SOUR
- [ ] HERBAL
- [ ] OILY
- [ ] LEATHER

FLAVOR STRENGTH

(1) (2) (3) (4) (5) (6) (7) (8) (9) (10)

NOTES

....
....
....

WOULD YOU TRY AGAIN?

- [ ] YES
- [ ] NO

OVERALL RATING

★ ★ ★ ★ ★

Cigar Tasting Journal

NAME OF CIGAR

DATE   **ORIGIN**

BRAND   **TYPE**

WRAPPER   **FILLER**

SAMPLED   **LENGTH / RING SIZE**

PLACE CIGAR LABLE HERE

FLAVOR

☐ BITTER ☐ CREAMY ☐ FRUITY
☐ SPICY ☐ CHOCOLATE ☐ SOUR
☐ WOODY ☐ TOFFEE ☐ HERBAL
☐ EARTHY ☐ SWEET ☐ OILY
☐ NUTTY ☐ FLORAL ☐ LEATHER

FLAVOR STRENGTH

① ② ③ ④ ⑤ ⑥ ⑦ ⑧ ⑨ ⑩

NOTES

....
....
....

WOULD YOU TRY AGAIN?

☐ YES ☐ NO

OVERALL RATING

★ ★ ★ ★ ★

Cigar Tasting Journal

NAME OF CIGAR

DATE   **ORIGIN**

BRAND   **TYPE**

WRAPPER   **FILLER**

SAMPLED   **LENGTH / RING SIZE**

PLACE CIGAR LABLE HERE

FLAVOR

☐ BITTER   ☐ CREAMY   ☐ FRUITY
☐ SPICY   ☐ CHOCOLATE   ☐ SOUR
☐ WOODY   ☐ TOFFEE   ☐ HERBAL
☐ EARTHY   ☐ SWEET   ☐ OILY
☐ NUTTY   ☐ FLORAL   ☐ LEATHER

FLAVOR STRENGTH

① ② ③ ④ ⑤ ⑥ ⑦ ⑧ ⑨ ⑩

NOTES

....
....
....

WOULD YOU TRY AGAIN?   **OVERALL RATING**

☐ YES   ☐ NO   ⭐ ⭐ ⭐ ⭐ ⭐

Cigar Tasting Journal

NAME OF CIGAR

DATE   **ORIGIN**

BRAND   **TYPE**

WRAPPER   **FILLER**

SAMPLED   **LENGTH / RING SIZE**

PLACE CIGAR LABLE HERE

FLAVOR

- ☐ BITTER
- ☐ SPICY
- ☐ WOODY
- ☐ EARTHY
- ☐ NUTTY
- ☐ CREAMY
- ☐ CHOCOLATE
- ☐ TOFFEE
- ☐ SWEET
- ☐ FLORAL
- ☐ FRUITY
- ☐ SOUR
- ☐ HERBAL
- ☐ OILY
- ☐ LEATHER

FLAVOR STRENGTH

① ② ③ ④ ⑤ ⑥ ⑦ ⑧ ⑨ ⑩

NOTES

....
....
....

WOULD YOU TRY AGAIN?   **OVERALL RATING**

☐ YES   ☐ NO   ★★★★★

Cigar Tasting Journal

NAME OF CIGAR

DATE   **ORIGIN**

BRAND   **TYPE**

WRAPPER   **FILLER**

SAMPLED   **LENGTH / RING SIZE**

PLACE CIGAR LABLE HERE

FLAVOR

- ☐ BITTER
- ☐ SPICY
- ☐ WOODY
- ☐ EARTHY
- ☐ NUTTY

- ☐ CREAMY
- ☐ CHOCOLATE
- ☐ TOFFEE
- ☐ SWEET
- ☐ FLORAL

- ☐ FRUITY
- ☐ SOUR
- ☐ HERBAL
- ☐ OILY
- ☐ LEATHER

FLAVOR STRENGTH

① ② ③ ④ ⑤ ⑥ ⑦ ⑧ ⑨ ⑩

NOTES

....
....
....

WOULD YOU TRY AGAIN?   **OVERALL RATING**

☐ YES   ☐ NO   ☆ ☆ ☆ ☆ ☆

Cigar Tasting Journal

NAME OF CIGAR

DATE   **ORIGIN**

BRAND   **TYPE**

WRAPPER   **FILLER**

SAMPLED   **LENGTH / RING SIZE**

PLACE CIGAR LABLE HERE

FLAVOR

- ☐ BITTER
- ☐ SPICY
- ☐ WOODY
- ☐ EARTHY
- ☐ NUTTY

- ☐ CREAMY
- ☐ CHOCOLATE
- ☐ TOFFEE
- ☐ SWEET
- ☐ FLORAL

- ☐ FRUITY
- ☐ SOUR
- ☐ HERBAL
- ☐ OILY
- ☐ LEATHER

FLAVOR STRENGTH

① ② ③ ④ ⑤ ⑥ ⑦ ⑧ ⑨ ⑩

NOTES

....
....
....

WOULD YOU TRY AGAIN?   **OVERALL RATING**

☐ YES   ☐ NO   ⭐ ⭐ ⭐ ⭐ ⭐

Cigar Tasting Journal

NAME OF CIGAR

DATE   **ORIGIN**

BRAND   **TYPE**

WRAPPER   **FILLER**

SAMPLED   **LENGTH / RING SIZE**

PLACE CIGAR LABLE HERE

FLAVOR

- ☐ BITTER
- ☐ SPICY
- ☐ WOODY
- ☐ EARTHY
- ☐ NUTTY
- ☐ CREAMY
- ☐ CHOCOLATE
- ☐ TOFFEE
- ☐ SWEET
- ☐ FLORAL
- ☐ FRUITY
- ☐ SOUR
- ☐ HERBAL
- ☐ OILY
- ☐ LEATHER

FLAVOR STRENGTH

① ② ③ ④ ⑤ ⑥ ⑦ ⑧ ⑨ ⑩

NOTES

....
....
....

WOULD YOU TRY AGAIN?   **OVERALL RATING**

☐ YES   ☐ NO   ⭐ ⭐ ⭐ ⭐ ⭐

Cigar Tasting Journal

NAME OF CIGAR

DATE　　　　　　　　　　　**ORIGIN**

BRAND　　　　　　　　　　**TYPE**

WRAPPER　　　　　　　　　**FILLER**

SAMPLED　　　　　　　　　**LENGTH / RING SIZE**

PLACE CIGAR LABLE HERE

FLAVOR

☐ BITTER ☐ CREAMY ☐ FRUITY
☐ SPICY ☐ CHOCOLATE ☐ SOUR
☐ WOODY ☐ TOFFEE ☐ HERBAL
☐ EARTHY ☐ SWEET ☐ OILY
☐ NUTTY ☐ FLORAL ☐ LEATHER

FLAVOR STRENGTH

① ② ③ ④ ⑤ ⑥ ⑦ ⑧ ⑨ ⑩

NOTES

....
....
....

WOULD YOU TRY AGAIN?　　　　**OVERALL RATING**

☐ YES　　☐ NO　　　　★ ★ ★ ★ ★

Cigar Tasting Journal

NAME OF CIGAR

DATE   **ORIGIN**

BRAND   **TYPE**

WRAPPER   **FILLER**

SAMPLED   **LENGTH / RING SIZE**

PLACE CIGAR LABLE HERE

FLAVOR

- ☐ BITTER
- ☐ SPICY
- ☐ WOODY
- ☐ EARTHY
- ☐ NUTTY

- ☐ CREAMY
- ☐ CHOCOLATE
- ☐ TOFFEE
- ☐ SWEET
- ☐ FLORAL

- ☐ FRUITY
- ☐ SOUR
- ☐ HERBAL
- ☐ OILY
- ☐ LEATHER

FLAVOR STRENGTH

① ② ③ ④ ⑤ ⑥ ⑦ ⑧ ⑨ ⑩

NOTES

··
··
··

WOULD YOU TRY AGAIN?

☐ YES   ☐ NO

OVERALL RATING

★ ★ ★ ★ ★

Cigar Tasting Journal

NAME OF CIGAR

DATE   **ORIGIN**

BRAND   **TYPE**

WRAPPER   **FILLER**

SAMPLED   **LENGTH / RING SIZE**

PLACE CIGAR LABLE HERE

FLAVOR

- ☐ BITTER
- ☐ SPICY
- ☐ WOODY
- ☐ EARTHY
- ☐ NUTTY
- ☐ CREAMY
- ☐ CHOCOLATE
- ☐ TOFFEE
- ☐ SWEET
- ☐ FLORAL
- ☐ FRUITY
- ☐ SOUR
- ☐ HERBAL
- ☐ OILY
- ☐ LEATHER

FLAVOR STRENGTH

① ② ③ ④ ⑤ ⑥ ⑦ ⑧ ⑨ ⑩

NOTES

....
....
....

WOULD YOU TRY AGAIN?   **OVERALL RATING**

☐ YES   ☐ NO   ★ ★ ★ ★ ★

Cigar Tasting Journal

NAME OF CIGAR

DATE **ORIGIN**

BRAND **TYPE**

WRAPPER **FILLER**

SAMPLED **LENGTH / RING SIZE**

PLACE CIGAR LABLE HERE

FLAVOR

- [ ] BITTER
- [ ] SPICY
- [ ] WOODY
- [ ] EARTHY
- [ ] NUTTY
- [ ] CREAMY
- [ ] CHOCOLATE
- [ ] TOFFEE
- [ ] SWEET
- [ ] FLORAL
- [ ] FRUITY
- [ ] SOUR
- [ ] HERBAL
- [ ] OILY
- [ ] LEATHER

FLAVOR STRENGTH

(1) (2) (3) (4) (5) (6) (7) (8) (9) (10)

NOTES

....
....
....

WOULD YOU TRY AGAIN?

- [ ] YES
- [ ] NO

OVERALL RATING

★ ★ ★ ★ ★

Cigar Tasting Journal

NAME OF CIGAR

DATE　　　　　　　　　　　　**ORIGIN**

BRAND　　　　　　　　　　　**TYPE**

WRAPPER　　　　　　　　　**FILLER**

SAMPLED　　　　　　　　　**LENGTH / RING SIZE**

PLACE CIGAR LABLE HERE

FLAVOR

- ☐ BITTER
- ☐ SPICY
- ☐ WOODY
- ☐ EARTHY
- ☐ NUTTY
- ☐ CREAMY
- ☐ CHOCOLATE
- ☐ TOFFEE
- ☐ SWEET
- ☐ FLORAL
- ☐ FRUITY
- ☐ SOUR
- ☐ HERBAL
- ☐ OILY
- ☐ LEATHER

FLAVOR STRENGTH

① ② ③ ④ ⑤ ⑥ ⑦ ⑧ ⑨ ⑩

NOTES

....
....
....

WOULD YOU TRY AGAIN?

☐ YES　　　☐ NO

OVERALL RATING

☆ ☆ ☆ ☆ ☆

Cigar Tasting Journal

NAME OF CIGAR

DATE   **ORIGIN**

BRAND   **TYPE**

WRAPPER   **FILLER**

SAMPLED   **LENGTH / RING SIZE**

PLACE CIGAR LABLE HERE

FLAVOR

☐ BITTER   ☐ CREAMY   ☐ FRUITY
☐ SPICY   ☐ CHOCOLATE   ☐ SOUR
☐ WOODY   ☐ TOFFEE   ☐ HERBAL
☐ EARTHY   ☐ SWEET   ☐ OILY
☐ NUTTY   ☐ FLORAL   ☐ LEATHER

FLAVOR STRENGTH

① ② ③ ④ ⑤ ⑥ ⑦ ⑧ ⑨ ⑩

NOTES

....
....
....

WOULD YOU TRY AGAIN?   **OVERALL RATING**

☐ YES   ☐ NO   ⭐ ⭐ ⭐ ⭐ ⭐

Cigar Tasting Journal

NAME OF CIGAR

DATE   **ORIGIN**

BRAND   **TYPE**

WRAPPER   **FILLER**

SAMPLED   **LENGTH / RING SIZE**

PLACE CIGAR LABLE HERE

FLAVOR

- ☐ BITTER
- ☐ SPICY
- ☐ WOODY
- ☐ EARTHY
- ☐ NUTTY

- ☐ CREAMY
- ☐ CHOCOLATE
- ☐ TOFFEE
- ☐ SWEET
- ☐ FLORAL

- ☐ FRUITY
- ☐ SOUR
- ☐ HERBAL
- ☐ OILY
- ☐ LEATHER

FLAVOR STRENGTH

① ② ③ ④ ⑤ ⑥ ⑦ ⑧ ⑨ ⑩

NOTES

....
....
....

WOULD YOU TRY AGAIN?   **OVERALL RATING**

☐ YES   ☐ NO   ☆ ☆ ☆ ☆ ☆

Cigar Tasting Journal

NAME OF CIGAR

DATE		**ORIGIN**	
BRAND		**TYPE**	
WRAPPER		**FILLER**	
SAMPLED		**LENGTH / RING SIZE**	

PLACE CIGAR LABLE HERE

FLAVOR

- ☐ BITTER
- ☐ SPICY
- ☐ WOODY
- ☐ EARTHY
- ☐ NUTTY
- ☐ CREAMY
- ☐ CHOCOLATE
- ☐ TOFFEE
- ☐ SWEET
- ☐ FLORAL
- ☐ FRUITY
- ☐ SOUR
- ☐ HERBAL
- ☐ OILY
- ☐ LEATHER

FLAVOR STRENGTH

① ② ③ ④ ⑤ ⑥ ⑦ ⑧ ⑨ ⑩

NOTES

....
....
....

WOULD YOU TRY AGAIN?

☐ YES   ☐ NO

OVERALL RATING

★ ★ ★ ★ ★

Cigar Tasting Journal

NAME OF CIGAR

DATE   **ORIGIN**

BRAND   **TYPE**

WRAPPER   **FILLER**

SAMPLED   **LENGTH / RING SIZE**

PLACE CIGAR LABLE HERE

FLAVOR

☐ BITTER   ☐ CREAMY   ☐ FRUITY
☐ SPICY   ☐ CHOCOLATE   ☐ SOUR
☐ WOODY   ☐ TOFFEE   ☐ HERBAL
☐ EARTHY   ☐ SWEET   ☐ OILY
☐ NUTTY   ☐ FLORAL   ☐ LEATHER

FLAVOR STRENGTH

① ② ③ ④ ⑤ ⑥ ⑦ ⑧ ⑨ ⑩

NOTES

....
....
....

WOULD YOU TRY AGAIN?   **OVERALL RATING**

☐ YES   ☐ NO   ★ ★ ★ ★ ★

Cigar Tasting Journal

NAME OF CIGAR

DATE

ORIGIN

BRAND

TYPE

WRAPPER

FILLER

SAMPLED

LENGTH / RING SIZE

PLACE CIGAR LABLE HERE

FLAVOR

- [ ] BITTER
- [ ] SPICY
- [ ] WOODY
- [ ] EARTHY
- [ ] NUTTY
- [ ] CREAMY
- [ ] CHOCOLATE
- [ ] TOFFEE
- [ ] SWEET
- [ ] FLORAL
- [ ] FRUITY
- [ ] SOUR
- [ ] HERBAL
- [ ] OILY
- [ ] LEATHER

FLAVOR STRENGTH

(1) (2) (3) (4) (5) (6) (7) (8) (9) (10)

NOTES

....
....
....

WOULD YOU TRY AGAIN?

- [ ] YES
- [ ] NO

OVERALL RATING

★ ★ ★ ★ ★

Cigar Tasting Journal

NAME OF CIGAR

DATE   **ORIGIN**

BRAND   **TYPE**

WRAPPER   **FILLER**

SAMPLED   **LENGTH / RING SIZE**

PLACE CIGAR LABLE HERE

FLAVOR

☐ BITTER   ☐ CREAMY   ☐ FRUITY
☐ SPICY   ☐ CHOCOLATE   ☐ SOUR
☐ WOODY   ☐ TOFFEE   ☐ HERBAL
☐ EARTHY   ☐ SWEET   ☐ OILY
☐ NUTTY   ☐ FLORAL   ☐ LEATHER

FLAVOR STRENGTH

① ② ③ ④ ⑤ ⑥ ⑦ ⑧ ⑨ ⑩

NOTES

....
....
....

WOULD YOU TRY AGAIN?   ## OVERALL RATING

☐ YES   ☐ NO   ★ ★ ★ ★ ★

Cigar Tasting Journal

NAME OF CIGAR

DATE   **ORIGIN**

BRAND   **TYPE**

WRAPPER   **FILLER**

SAMPLED   **LENGTH / RING SIZE**

PLACE CIGAR LABLE HERE

FLAVOR

- ☐ BITTER
- ☐ SPICY
- ☐ WOODY
- ☐ EARTHY
- ☐ NUTTY

- ☐ CREAMY
- ☐ CHOCOLATE
- ☐ TOFFEE
- ☐ SWEET
- ☐ FLORAL

- ☐ FRUITY
- ☐ SOUR
- ☐ HERBAL
- ☐ OILY
- ☐ LEATHER

FLAVOR STRENGTH

① ② ③ ④ ⑤ ⑥ ⑦ ⑧ ⑨ ⑩

NOTES

....
....
....

WOULD YOU TRY AGAIN?   **OVERALL RATING**

☐ YES   ☐ NO   ⭐ ⭐ ⭐ ⭐ ⭐

Cigar Tasting Journal

NAME OF CIGAR

DATE   **ORIGIN**

BRAND   **TYPE**

WRAPPER   **FILLER**

SAMPLED   **LENGTH / RING SIZE**

PLACE CIGAR LABLE HERE

FLAVOR

- ☐ BITTER
- ☐ SPICY
- ☐ WOODY
- ☐ EARTHY
- ☐ NUTTY
- ☐ CREAMY
- ☐ CHOCOLATE
- ☐ TOFFEE
- ☐ SWEET
- ☐ FLORAL
- ☐ FRUITY
- ☐ SOUR
- ☐ HERBAL
- ☐ OILY
- ☐ LEATHER

FLAVOR STRENGTH

① ② ③ ④ ⑤ ⑥ ⑦ ⑧ ⑨ ⑩

NOTES

....
....
....

WOULD YOU TRY AGAIN?

☐ YES   ☐ NO

OVERALL RATING

★ ★ ★ ★ ★

Cigar Tasting Journal

NAME OF CIGAR

DATE   **ORIGIN**

BRAND   **TYPE**

WRAPPER   **FILLER**

SAMPLED   **LENGTH / RING SIZE**

PLACE CIGAR LABLE HERE

FLAVOR

- ☐ BITTER
- ☐ SPICY
- ☐ WOODY
- ☐ EARTHY
- ☐ NUTTY
- ☐ CREAMY
- ☐ CHOCOLATE
- ☐ TOFFEE
- ☐ SWEET
- ☐ FLORAL
- ☐ FRUITY
- ☐ SOUR
- ☐ HERBAL
- ☐ OILY
- ☐ LEATHER

FLAVOR STRENGTH

① ② ③ ④ ⑤ ⑥ ⑦ ⑧ ⑨ ⑩

NOTES

....
....
....

WOULD YOU TRY AGAIN?

☐ YES   ☐ NO

OVERALL RATING

★ ★ ★ ★ ★

Cigar Tasting Journal

NAME OF CIGAR

DATE   ORIGIN

BRAND   TYPE

WRAPPER   FILLER

SAMPLED   LENGTH / RING SIZE

PLACE CIGAR LABLE HERE

FLAVOR

- ☐ BITTER
- ☐ SPICY
- ☐ WOODY
- ☐ EARTHY
- ☐ NUTTY
- ☐ CREAMY
- ☐ CHOCOLATE
- ☐ TOFFEE
- ☐ SWEET
- ☐ FLORAL
- ☐ FRUITY
- ☐ SOUR
- ☐ HERBAL
- ☐ OILY
- ☐ LEATHER

FLAVOR STRENGTH

① ② ③ ④ ⑤ ⑥ ⑦ ⑧ ⑨ ⑩

NOTES

WOULD YOU TRY AGAIN?

☐ YES   ☐ NO

OVERALL RATING

★ ★ ★ ★ ★

Cigar Tasting Journal

NAME OF CIGAR

DATE   **ORIGIN**

BRAND   **TYPE**

WRAPPER   **FILLER**

SAMPLED   **LENGTH / RING SIZE**

PLACE CIGAR LABLE HERE

FLAVOR

☐ BITTER   ☐ CREAMY   ☐ FRUITY
☐ SPICY   ☐ CHOCOLATE   ☐ SOUR
☐ WOODY   ☐ TOFFEE   ☐ HERBAL
☐ EARTHY   ☐ SWEET   ☐ OILY
☐ NUTTY   ☐ FLORAL   ☐ LEATHER

FLAVOR STRENGTH

① ② ③ ④ ⑤ ⑥ ⑦ ⑧ ⑨ ⑩

NOTES

....
....
....

WOULD YOU TRY AGAIN?   **OVERALL RATING**

☐ YES   ☐ NO   ★ ★ ★ ★ ★

Cigar Tasting Journal

NAME OF CIGAR

DATE   **ORIGIN**

BRAND   **TYPE**

WRAPPER   **FILLER**

SAMPLED   **LENGTH / RING SIZE**

PLACE CIGAR LABLE HERE

FLAVOR

☐ BITTER   ☐ CREAMY   ☐ FRUITY
☐ SPICY   ☐ CHOCOLATE   ☐ SOUR
☐ WOODY   ☐ TOFFEE   ☐ HERBAL
☐ EARTHY   ☐ SWEET   ☐ OILY
☐ NUTTY   ☐ FLORAL   ☐ LEATHER

FLAVOR STRENGTH

① ② ③ ④ ⑤ ⑥ ⑦ ⑧ ⑨ ⑩

NOTES

....
....
....

WOULD YOU TRY AGAIN?   ## OVERALL RATING

☐ YES   ☐ NO   ★ ★ ★ ★ ★

Cigar Tasting Journal

NAME OF CIGAR

DATE **ORIGIN**

BRAND **TYPE**

WRAPPER **FILLER**

SAMPLED **LENGTH / RING SIZE**

PLACE CIGAR LABLE HERE

FLAVOR

- [ ] BITTER
- [ ] SPICY
- [ ] WOODY
- [ ] EARTHY
- [ ] NUTTY
- [ ] CREAMY
- [ ] CHOCOLATE
- [ ] TOFFEE
- [ ] SWEET
- [ ] FLORAL
- [ ] FRUITY
- [ ] SOUR
- [ ] HERBAL
- [ ] OILY
- [ ] LEATHER

FLAVOR STRENGTH

(1) (2) (3) (4) (5) (6) (7) (8) (9) (10)

NOTES

....
....
....

WOULD YOU TRY AGAIN?

- [ ] YES
- [ ] NO

OVERALL RATING

☆ ☆ ☆ ☆ ☆

Cigar Tasting Journal

NAME OF CIGAR

DATE   ORIGIN

BRAND   TYPE

WRAPPER   FILLER

SAMPLED   LENGTH / RING SIZE

PLACE CIGAR LABLE HERE

FLAVOR

- [ ] BITTER
- [ ] SPICY
- [ ] WOODY
- [ ] EARTHY
- [ ] NUTTY
- [ ] CREAMY
- [ ] CHOCOLATE
- [ ] TOFFEE
- [ ] SWEET
- [ ] FLORAL
- [ ] FRUITY
- [ ] SOUR
- [ ] HERBAL
- [ ] OILY
- [ ] LEATHER

FLAVOR STRENGTH

(1) (2) (3) (4) (5) (6) (7) (8) (9) (10)

NOTES

....
....
....

WOULD YOU TRY AGAIN?

- [ ] YES
- [ ] NO

OVERALL RATING

★ ★ ★ ★ ★

Cigar Tasting Journal

NAME OF CIGAR

DATE
ORIGIN

BRAND
TYPE

WRAPPER
FILLER

SAMPLED
LENGTH / RING SIZE

PLACE CIGAR LABLE HERE

FLAVOR

- ☐ BITTER
- ☐ SPICY
- ☐ WOODY
- ☐ EARTHY
- ☐ NUTTY

- ☐ CREAMY
- ☐ CHOCOLATE
- ☐ TOFFEE
- ☐ SWEET
- ☐ FLORAL

- ☐ FRUITY
- ☐ SOUR
- ☐ HERBAL
- ☐ OILY
- ☐ LEATHER

FLAVOR STRENGTH

① ② ③ ④ ⑤ ⑥ ⑦ ⑧ ⑨ ⑩

NOTES

....
....
....

WOULD YOU TRY AGAIN?
☐ YES ☐ NO

OVERALL RATING
★ ★ ★ ★ ★

Cigar Tasting Journal

NAME OF CIGAR

DATE

ORIGIN

BRAND

TYPE

WRAPPER

FILLER

SAMPLED

LENGTH / RING SIZE

PLACE CIGAR LABLE HERE

FLAVOR

- ☐ BITTER
- ☐ SPICY
- ☐ WOODY
- ☐ EARTHY
- ☐ NUTTY
- ☐ CREAMY
- ☐ CHOCOLATE
- ☐ TOFFEE
- ☐ SWEET
- ☐ FLORAL
- ☐ FRUITY
- ☐ SOUR
- ☐ HERBAL
- ☐ OILY
- ☐ LEATHER

FLAVOR STRENGTH

① ② ③ ④ ⑤ ⑥ ⑦ ⑧ ⑨ ⑩

NOTES

....
....
....

WOULD YOU TRY AGAIN?

☐ YES   ☐ NO

OVERALL RATING

★ ★ ★ ★ ★

Cigar Tasting Journal

NAME OF CIGAR

DATE   **ORIGIN**

BRAND   **TYPE**

WRAPPER   **FILLER**

SAMPLED   **LENGTH / RING SIZE**

PLACE CIGAR LABLE HERE

FLAVOR

- ☐ BITTER
- ☐ SPICY
- ☐ WOODY
- ☐ EARTHY
- ☐ NUTTY

- ☐ CREAMY
- ☐ CHOCOLATE
- ☐ TOFFEE
- ☐ SWEET
- ☐ FLORAL

- ☐ FRUITY
- ☐ SOUR
- ☐ HERBAL
- ☐ OILY
- ☐ LEATHER

FLAVOR STRENGTH

① ② ③ ④ ⑤ ⑥ ⑦ ⑧ ⑨ ⑩

NOTES

....
....
....

WOULD YOU TRY AGAIN?   **OVERALL RATING**

☐ YES   ☐ NO   ★ ★ ★ ★ ★

Cigar Tasting Journal

NAME OF CIGAR

DATE   **ORIGIN**

BRAND   **TYPE**

WRAPPER   **FILLER**

SAMPLED   **LENGTH / RING SIZE**

PLACE CIGAR LABLE HERE

FLAVOR

- ☐ BITTER
- ☐ SPICY
- ☐ WOODY
- ☐ EARTHY
- ☐ NUTTY
- ☐ CREAMY
- ☐ CHOCOLATE
- ☐ TOFFEE
- ☐ SWEET
- ☐ FLORAL
- ☐ FRUITY
- ☐ SOUR
- ☐ HERBAL
- ☐ OILY
- ☐ LEATHER

FLAVOR STRENGTH

① ② ③ ④ ⑤ ⑥ ⑦ ⑧ ⑨ ⑩

NOTES

....
....
....

WOULD YOU TRY AGAIN?   **OVERALL RATING**

☐ YES   ☐ NO   ☆ ☆ ☆ ☆ ☆

Cigar Tasting Journal

NAME OF CIGAR

DATE **ORIGIN**

BRAND **TYPE**

WRAPPER **FILLER**

SAMPLED **LENGTH / RING SIZE**

PLACE CIGAR LABLE HERE

FLAVOR

- [ ] BITTER
- [ ] SPICY
- [ ] WOODY
- [ ] EARTHY
- [ ] NUTTY
- [ ] CREAMY
- [ ] CHOCOLATE
- [ ] TOFFEE
- [ ] SWEET
- [ ] FLORAL
- [ ] FRUITY
- [ ] SOUR
- [ ] HERBAL
- [ ] OILY
- [ ] LEATHER

FLAVOR STRENGTH

(1) (2) (3) (4) (5) (6) (7) (8) (9) (10)

NOTES

....
....
....

WOULD YOU TRY AGAIN?
- [ ] YES
- [ ] NO

OVERALL RATING
⭐ ⭐ ⭐ ⭐ ⭐

Cigar Tasting Journal

NAME OF CIGAR

DATE   **ORIGIN**

BRAND   **TYPE**

WRAPPER   **FILLER**

SAMPLED   **LENGTH / RING SIZE**

PLACE CIGAR LABLE HERE

FLAVOR

- ☐ BITTER
- ☐ SPICY
- ☐ WOODY
- ☐ EARTHY
- ☐ NUTTY
- ☐ CREAMY
- ☐ CHOCOLATE
- ☐ TOFFEE
- ☐ SWEET
- ☐ FLORAL
- ☐ FRUITY
- ☐ SOUR
- ☐ HERBAL
- ☐ OILY
- ☐ LEATHER

FLAVOR STRENGTH

① ② ③ ④ ⑤ ⑥ ⑦ ⑧ ⑨ ⑩

NOTES

....
....
....

WOULD YOU TRY AGAIN?

☐ YES   ☐ NO

OVERALL RATING

★ ★ ★ ★ ★

Printed in Great Britain
by Amazon